# RE-INVENTION OF LIBRARIANSHIP

Its Multiple Facets

# RE-INVENTION OF LIBRARIANSHIP

## Its Multiple Facets

**L.S. Ramaiah**

**Ess Ess Publications**
New Delhi

***RE-INVENTION OF LIBRARIANSHIP***
***Its Multiple Facets***



**ISBN: 978-81-7000-612-1**

**Rs.700/-**

**First Published 2010**

Published by:
**Ess Ess Publications**
4837/24, Ansari Road,
Darya Ganj,
New Delhi-110 002.
INDIA
Phones: 23260807, 41563444
Fax: 41563334
E-mail: info@essessreference.com
www.essessreference.com

Cover Design by *Patch Creative Unit*

Printed and bound in India at Salasar Imaging Systems.

*Dedicated to*
*My Daughter*
**Smt. M. Nagalakshmi**
*with love for her truthfulness, honesty*
*forbearence and courage*

*Let nothing upset you,*
*Let nothing frighten you,*
*Everything is changing,*
*God alone is changeless,*
*Patience attains the goal,*
*Who has God lacks nothing;*
*God alone fills everyneed.*

# CONTENTS

# Acknowledgements

Acknowledgements is a formality in every book. It is impossible to acknowledge the help one gets from elders and friends who helped him to shape his personality. The influences are so many from so many people from birth to death, it is impossible to compress them into a para. Out of the people who caused million mutinies in us atleast some cannot be avoided from narration.

First of all I am greatful to my parents and family who gave birth to me and sustained me. My sincere thanks are due to late Prof. Ramesh Mohan, former Vice Chancellor of the Central Institute of English and Foreign languages which is renamed recently as the English and Foreign languages University, Hyderabad. I am indebted to many persons at this University for their ideas. They are late. Prof. S. K. Verma, Prof. V.D. Singh, Prof. R.N. Ghosh, late Dr. S.R. Ganguly, Prof. Dimri, Prof. Krishnaswamy, Prof. Pradhan, Late Prof. K. Subramanian, Prof. V. Prakasam. I extend my grateful thanks to all of them.

There are many friends to me in the LIS Profession all over India. Among them I sincerely extend my thanks to Prof. A.A.N. Raju, Prof. G.V.S.L.N. Raju, Prof. K. Sarada, Prof. Guruswamy Naidu, Prof. Mangla, Prof. Girija Kumar, Dr. Pandey K.Sharma, Dr. Jayati Ghosh, Shri. K.K. Banerjee, Prof. N.R. Satyanarayana, Dr. M. Sankara Reddy and Shri Tummala Ashok Babu.

Finally, I express my thanks to my publishers, Mr. R. Seshadri, former proprieter of M/s. T. R. Publications, Chennai and Mr. Sumit Sethi, a friend and an eminent publisher of LIS publications in the country of M/s. Ess Ess Publications, New Delhi for their interest, help and encouragement in publishing my books.

**L.S. Ramaiah**

# Introduction

*"The great thing about a computer note book is that no matter how much you stuff into it, it does not get bigger or heavier."*
**– Bill Gates.**

Ideas are like atoms. They are small when they generate in the human brain. It is not known how they generate. Saplings as they generate from small seeds, and then grow, develop branches and yield flowers and fruits; the ideas also grow into sentences, paragraphs, chapters and books and develop information, knowledge and wisdom. The breath and width of information has been constantly expanding without bounds. Between the earth and the sky, there is no place where information is absent. Information is catalyst in the development and progress of Human Civilization. Information and its seminal product Knowledge are putting the humans to other planets in the universe. The space machines will shuttle between the earth and the other planets. A day is not far away when the humans to establish habitats and digital information centres (libraries) beyond this world and in other worlds.

Libraries were there in the past. Libraries like the Alexandrian Library, the Nalanda and the Takshasila Libraries, the Imperial Library of the Moghuls and the British Museem Library had historic significance. Valtaire and Karl Marx through their geniuses and ideas in their writings prepared the background for revolutions. The French, American and Russian Revolutions recognised the human values. They brought a tunning point in human history. Sciences began to develp. Libraries and Information became the handmaids of science. Roots were laid for libraries and library science in the 19th century and the 20th century witnessed the emergence of Information science. The library and information science is no longer a 'Little Science' of yester-years. It has become a "Major Science" and science of all sciences. In developed countries, the governments have recognised the libraries and information as a major sector in their plans. They have National Information Polices.

What is the position of libraries and information in India? It is dismal. There is no National Policy. The National Policy draft is languishing in the government files for more than two decades. The National Library and its three Deposit Centres are in chaotic condition. They don't receive all the books published in India as per the Delivery of Books Act (1954). Prof. A.A.N. Raju said in his recent book, *Legal Deposit and Bibliographical Control in India* (2009) that "no more than 30% to 40% of the books published in the country are deposited at the National Library, Kolkata." It shows clearly that the National Library has failed in carrying out one of its important functions. It clearly displays that the bibliographic control in the country is completely inadequate. The National Knowledge Commission in its publication, *Libraries, Gateways to Knowledge. A road map for revitalization* (2007) said that there should be a paradigm shift in the country to overcome "information poverty" in Libraries and Information sector.

The provision and position of the public libraries in the country is further dismal. According to the Constitution of our Republic, the subject libraries is in the state list of powers. There is uneven growth of libraries in the states due to lack of common policy and direction. India in 28 states and 7 union terrotories with more than a billion population living in 3,366 cities and towns and 5,57,137 villages, the extent of libraries are 30 states, central libraries, 40 regional libraries, 364 district libraries, 4658 city and town libraries and 49758 village libraries. The total strength of libraries, both urban and rural is 54,851 only. 9% of villagers have public libraries. In terms of the expenditure per capita on public library is Re. 0.07. These statistics stated in the Nielson-Org-Marg Report submitted to the RRRLF, clearly reveal how the ruling governments in our country are fooling the people even after 60 years of Independence. Committees and Commissions like the Empowered committee, NAPLIS committee and Knowledge Commission and a galore of them were appointed from time to time. No action was taken on their recommendations. Governments while appointing committee after committee, comission after comission is doing what was done. Instead of doing the done, the government should act on the recommendations. Sans its action the entire exercise is unproductive.

India, according to our Planning Commission and government ads is a developing country. Its overarching aim is to transform it into a vibrant knowledge based society. Is it possible with such a insuffient and inadequate library and information infrastructure? There is no National policy and no National Network. Inspite of the computer revolution in the developed countries, the adoption of computers in our libraries, particularly in our public libraries is at snail's pace. Without a national network it is impossible to get information. It is easy to get information on the Internet from the Library of Congress or the British National Library than from our National Library, Kolkata. People are starving for information.

From Warren Edward Buffet to village begger and from Prime Minister to Pauper everyone would need information in their everyday activity. Innocence leads to ignorance and ignorance is suicidal.

This small book of articles contains ideas on traditional

as well as modern topics in important areas of library and information science. An idea or two in the book may help the managers of Libraries and Information Centres at the time of need in their day to day work. It may be a good addition to your library collection.

Hyderabad, **L.S. Ramaiah**

15-08-09.

# 1

# KNOWLEDGE CULTURE

Ask a group of senior executives if they regard knowledge management as very important to the success of a company. Most will enthusiastically say that they do a response befitting one of the trendiest topics in management circles.

Yet thinking that knowledge management is crucial and knowing what to do about it are very different. Many executives think that knowledge management begins and ends with building sophisticated information technology systems.

Some companies go much further: they take the trouble to link all their information together and to build models that increase their profitability by improving processes, products, and customer relations. Such companies understand that true knowledge management requires them to develop ways of making workers aware of those links and goes beyond infrastructure to touch almost every aspect of a business.

## CREATING A DESIRE FOR KNOWLEDGE

Less successful companies tend to take a top-down approach: pushing knowledge to where it is needed. Successful companies, by contrast, reward employees for seeking, sharing, and creating knowledge. It requires effort to develop what we call "knowledge pull" - a grassroots desire among employees to tap into their company's intellectual resources. Almost all of the successful companies set ambitious goals for product development and process innovation.

Other techniques used by successful companies include granting financial and other incentives to reward employees who pull knowledge from internal and external sources and who contribute their own knowledge to the corporate base. Financial incentives can go a long way toward creating this kind of knowledge pull, but unless they are developed carefully they could encourage the hoarding of knowledge and other counterproductive practices. Incentive plans can also include coveted office space and other obvious status symbols as well as an opportunity to travel and to receive more challenging assignments.

Incentive systems should promote a broad range of corporate objectives, and successful companies tend to include knowledge management among them. Instead of focusing narrowly on individual performance, such companies ensure that incentives uphold a balanced range of goals that might include financial success outside an employee's immediate unit, for when people benefit from the success of other units in their companies, they are encouraged to move away from the knowledge-is-power mind-set and to begin sharing what they know. Other approaches, such as research competitions with high-prestige, high-value prizes, are more direct ways to encourage the sharing of knowledge.

The knowledge-pull mind-set can be created only if it becomes an integral part of corporate culture-a necessary first step before a company embarks on the more practical tasks of knowledge management.

## BRINGING KNOWLEDGE TO BEAR

Besides creating an environment that encourages knowledge pull, successful companies excel in applying, distributing, and creating knowledge-tasks that can't always be neatly separated. Dividing the range of knowledge-management practices among these three tasks is partly a matter of convenience and partly an attempt to distinguish techniques by the speed with which they can improve corporate performance. The three categories also help to identify areas in which a company's overall knowledge-management effort should be improved.

## APPLICATION

Every company is already sitting on a vast storehouse of knowledge but much of it is under used. The application of knowledge that is already in hand is the fastest and most direct way of using knowledge to influence a company's bottom line. Furthermore, if companies fail to apply knowledge, its successful distribution and cultivation will have little impact. Part of the problem is that "information" is generally a fact, whereas "knowledge." which focuses on linkages or relationships, is subjective. Each employee weighs knowledge against a different set of experiences and prejudices when deciding its meaning, value, and use. What is more, ideas can often be adapted to different processes or products, and successful companies actively try to apply knowledge to these new contexts. Some of the clearest examples of the way knowledge can be adapted come from companies that have searched far afield for new insights. A California construction company raised its rate of on-time cement deliveries to 95 percent, from 68 percent, by taking route-planning lessons from a local pizza delivery company.

## DISTRIBUTION

Techniques that benefit application often benefit distribution, since the two arc closely linked. But application focuses on using knowledge for immediate effect, distribution on moving knowledge to where it can best be applied. Distribution relies heavily on good infrastructure to create electronic meeting places, on databases, and on other channels for spreading knowledge.

However, successful companies-even those with IT systems facilitating smooth and broad exchanges of data-know that the challenge goes beyond building information networks. Much of a corporation's most valuable knowledge is tacit-embedded in the minds of employees. Tacit knowledge is difficult to manage, but successful companies have figured out ways to manage it. One global capital-goods company assigned product developers to the shop floor to supervise the production of the modules they had designed. This program opened up lines of communication between assembly-line employees and developers, thus giving the developers better insight into production problems, establishing continuing relations between the two groups, and encouraging the exchange of tacit knowledge between them. Within five years, the program, together with other measures, had cut production costs by 15 per cent and throughout time by 80 per cent.

## CREATION

Of all the tasks involved in managing knowledge, its creation is the most slippery, because creativity is cultivated rather than ordained. To remain vital, companies need new knowledge: ways of making paperwork run more smoothly say, or developing new products or services. New knowledge, moreover, is a necessary raw material for innovation, another strategic goal that partly overlaps with knowledge management. As Georg von Krogh has observed, "Knowledge creation is the key source of innovation in any company. Innovation and the creation of knowledge both closely tied to new-products and services-can often be sparked by similar techniques."

Our survey showed that successful companies often tried to foster creativity by making the jobs of employees more interesting for instance, by allowing employees to participate in projects not directly linked to their usual work. Eighty per cent of the successful companies, as compared with only 40 per cent of the less successful ones, had programs to encourage creativity, such as idea contests and opportunities to work on diverse projects. Means of access (such as fast Internet connections) to a wide range of external stimuli were available at 73 per cent of the successful companies.

Sometimes even bald-faced gimmicks work. One global electronics company developed a so-called virtual Hollywood and asked "directors" (employees) to present "scripts" (improvement ideas) to "investors" (general managers) who would choose the ones to "produce" (implement). The project promoted out-of-the-box thinking and in the first year generated submissions from 200 teams addressing process improvement and product development.

# 2

# The Need for Change in The Role of Public Libraries in India

## INTRODUCTION

India is a vast country with 28 states, 7 union territories, 3366 towns and cities, 5,57,130 villages with a population of more than a billion. It is one of the biggest democracies in the world. For the survival of the democracy, informed citizenry is essential. Education and public information system, (Public Libraries) are two pillars for the growth and development of the nation. Out of the two, Government of India has taken care to provide maximum importance through its plans to provide increased educational facilities. Today literacy has increased to 62%. Whereas the public library system or public libraries which provide sustainable information are lagging behind. There are only about 65000 libraries in the country which serve 5,57,130 villages. The present public libraries are also confined to urban areas like cities, towns and big villages. It is clearly evident that the public library system has not reached to the rural areas which are the heart of India. These days every village is provided with a school, bus, road, electricity, protected water system and many other physical facilities but the public library which is the intellectual component of education is conspicuously absent. Why not every village and hamlet be provided with a public library?

## CHANGING INDIA

No society is static. India today is not India of 1947. Some of the facets of change in modern society is evident in the following issues:

- Explosion of population bringing pressure on various segments of society.
- Economic growth effecting income, prices, value, culture and occupational situations
- Political changes changing the structure of the society in sharing power.
- Educational changes bringing increased number of schools, colleges, and universities.
- Growth of research, industries and business in every sector of life.
- Cultural changes in contact with other advanced societies.
- Changes in the mass media and communication like Telephones, Radio, Television, Newspapers etc.

## CHANGING REQUIREMENTS OF THE PEOPLE

With the above changes in society many challenges are confronted by individuals and groups at all levels of the society. People want more and more information to tackle their problems instead of borrowing books for their leisure reading. Till today the main activity of our public libraries is to check-out and check-in of books. They are like book museums. They hardly provide any information services, reference services and specialized information services. The present need of the public libraries is to provide information rather than books which contain information. Information is power. It is required in every sector of individuals' life both of the educated and illiterates.

Absence of current information makes them obsolete. The public libraries which are peoples universities should provide the required information to meet today's challenges and to solve their social and individual problems.

## NEED FOR MODERIZATION OF PUBLIC LIBRARIES

In advanced countries the public libraries are no longer like islands. They are linked together throughout width and breadth of their countries to get information from anywhere. But the position of public libraries in India has not changed at all for the last 62 years of our independence. Each library does not know what the other library has. There are networks in educational institutions, research institutions etc. We have INFLIBNET, DELNET, CALIBNET, RAILNET, NICNET etc. But so far the national library and other public libraries are not connected by any network. There is an urgent need to create a public library network to provide information to every individual what ever he needs. Computers and Information Technology are pervading into every sector of the society. People at large have become computer humans. Computer should be introduced in public library system in order to provide the muscle and strength to face the challenging and changing requirements of the society. If the new technology is not adopted as early as possible, our public libraries will remain like book-dens. People will hardly visit them except a few who spend their leisure time for reading newspapers. The modern formats of documents like e-Journals, e-Books, CDs , DVDs, Floppies etc., are absent in our public libraries. This will create a big hiatus between the readers in public libraries and the users of academic and special libraries. Modernization of public libraries, therefore, is the urgent need of the hour. Otherwise in a short time there will be no readers in our libraries. This will be handy to administrators to argue against the development and expansion of public libraries.

## FUNDS AND FINANCES

Public libraries are not spreading as fast as public educational institutions due to lack of proper and adequate funds. The state governments, due to lack of financial resources are not able to introduce library legislation in 17 states out of 28. Big states like, MP, J & K, Assam, Punjab etc., which constitute more than half of the population of India could not enact the library legislation fearing the financial glut. The growth and development of public libraries is the responsibility of both the central and state governments equally as in the case of education.

The library cess is an outmoded practice. People are not in a position to pay such type of special taxes. The governments as they are providing budgets for education, pwd, health, sanitation etc. should also provide provision for public libraries in their annual budgets. It is strongly felt that every state government should provide atleast 10% of their budget and 5% in the central budget also should be provided for the development of public libraries. The central budgetary provision should be given to the states through the RRRLF on the basis of population instead of matching grants. The RRRLF and the central government should bring pressure on the states to enact the library legislation where ever the legislation is not there so far. The Library Associations also should create lobbies in the respective states to bring forward library legislation which is an important first requisite as per the Unesco Manifesto. Without finances and legislation, it is not possible to establish libraries in every habitation in the country.

## MANPOWER

The Department of Public Libraries should be headed by persons who have qualifications and experience in library field. Administrators, however good they are not fit for the public libraries in view of their lack of attitude and aptitude for this kind of service to the people. The manpower working in public libraries also should be trained in modern technologies and handling of information and instruments through intensive inservice courses. The village library should be handled by professional who has atleast BLISc qualification. In this context it may be pointed out that the library schools should revise their syllabi appropriately and include the courses in information technology and communication technology to prepare the right type of manpower needed in future.

## PUBLIC LIBRARIES AS COMMUNITY INFORMATION CENTRES

Public libraries to play their role should make survey of the different needs of people in their jurisdiction. They should provide all community information services such as agricultural, health, education, administrative development schemes and remove the distance between the authorities and people. They should act like a information pro for the public. They should attract people of different sections to their portals and disseminate information needed for the short term and long term requirements. As the university libraries are the heart of universities, the public library should be the hub of the community they serve.

Even in the states where library legislation is in vogue, there are not sufficient libraries. Many existing libraries also don't have staff to manage them. The village libraries generally work between 8 am to 1 pm and 4pm to 7pm. The timings are not convenient to the surrounding villagers and farmers. The timings should be changed to the requirements of the people. Otherwise they hardly find the libraries working when they visit them.

## CHANGE OF ATTITUDE

Unless the attitude of the people at the helm of affairs is changed, no significant change can be expected for overall development of the public libraries. For this, the management has to be convinced with the urgency and need of changing the public libraries for the better. With the advent of modern information technologies and their applications many public libraries world over have been under going a sea change for the better.

## CONCLUSION

1. Every village should be provided with a public library by the next decade.
2. Every public library should be provided with computers and information kioskos and touch screen technologies.
3. Facilities should be increased for the training and production of manpower.
4. Only persons with library qualifications and experience should be the Directors of the Department of public libraries.
5. The Department of public libraries of every state should have long term and short term plans as Ranganadhan planned earlier for the development of public libraries in India.
6. The Directors of public libraries and state governments, should identify tribal areas, and backward regions in their states to provide special library services for their appropriate development.
7. The provision of physical facilities such as houses, roads, buses, schools alone will not be sufficient for the needs of people in rural India, without public libraries and information centres. Man does not live by bread alone.

## REFERENCES

1. India. Planning Commission : Report of the working group of the planning commission on modernization of library services and informatics for the seventh five year plan, 1985-90. New Delhi, 1984 (Mimeo).
2. Jain, M.K. (Chief Editor) 50 years of library and information services in India, Delhi. Shipra Publication, 1998.
3. Balakrishnan, S and Paliwala, P.K. Public Library systems in India New Delhi, Anmol Publications, 2001.
4. Agrawal, S.P. (General Editor) Information India : 1997-98 & 98-99 Global view. New Delhi, Concept publishing company, 2002
5. Balakrishnan, S and Paliwala, P.K. Role of computers in Library Science, New Delhi, Anmol Publications, 2001.

# 3

# INFORMATION, LIBRARIES AND MASS MEDIA

## INTRODUCTION

*Homo Sapiens* are unique in many ways, when compared with other beings. Rene Descartes, the French Philosopher, rightly summed up the importance of the human beings when he said: *Cogito ergo sum* (I think, therefore, I am). Due to biogenetic revolution the homo sapiens were enabled to think, remember and talk. Thinking is the root of all human knowledge. Human beings communicate their feelings and ideas through *dhvani* (sound), *sangna* (gesture), *pada* (words) and *dhrusya* (picture). Marshall McLuhan, therefore, said that the medium is the message. All four modes are being used by people for communication. Language, however, has become the dominant mode of communication.

The communication process consists of four components. They are: (1) communicator, (2) Message, (3) Medium, and (4) Audience. Without any one of them the process of communication is incomplete. Communication takes place between one to one, one to many, many to one and many to many. The verbal communication can be in any of the following forms. They are: (1) Oral communication, (2) Written

Communication,. (3) Print Media, and (4) Electronic Media. Let us see each of the four communication practices briefly.

## ORAL COMMUNICATION

Oral communication is the oldest one which the humans adopted after they acquired speech and language. It is a communication by mouth. It has a limited reach. There are still many tribal communities like Koyas, Savaras etc who use only oral communication. They do not have written languages. The oral communication gets distorted when it passes from one individual to the other. Oral communication is used for conversation, discourses, seminars, conferences, meetings etc,

## WRITTEN COMMUNICATION

Most of the world's languages do not have writing systems but many do. Documents of the pre-Gutenberg era were hand written. They were written on stones, skins, metals, papyrus etc. In India *talapatras* and birch bark were used for writing. Paper became the common medium in the medieval times. Through writing. inscriptions and manuscripts were prepared. Such documents were collected in Manuscripts Libraries, Museums and Archival collections. This type of communication was a great improvement over the oral one.

## PRINT MEDIA

One of the most significant events in the human history was the invention of movable type in 1454 by Johann Gutenberg. This enabled man to produce any book in millions of copies. Printed books/documents began to be available to all in bulk. Modern libraries housing books and other documents came into existence. Printing made us to overcome the limitations of memory, space and time in dissemination of information.

## ELECTRONIC MEDIA

The Industrial Revolution and the subsequent

innovations like the Morse code, Telephone, Radio, Cinema and Television revolutionised the communication process. Machine became the extension of Man. The developments in telecommunication have made the world a global village. Technological and industrial innovations created the Mass Media in this century. Mass Media have become effective instruments for information dissemination and societal development.

## MASS MEDIA : NATURE AND SCOPE

The word 'Mass Media' is used collectively with reference to radio, television, cinema and the high-circulation news papers. The singular 'medium' means any agency which diffuses information to the public. The word 'media' is frequently used as a singular noun, and occasionally 'medias' as plural.

The earliest use of the term 'mass medium', as recorded in the Oxford English Dictionary (OED) 2nd. edn., was by S. M. Fechheimer in N.T. Prigg's *Advertising and Selling* (1923), at which time the one medium popularly known to the masses was the printed word, though radio broadcasting had just developed in the USA in 1922. The OED quotes J.S. Huxley in 1946: 'The media of mass communication - the somewhat cumbrous title (commonly abbreviated to Mass Media) proposed for agencies, such as the radio, the cinema and the popular press, which are capable of the mass dissemination of word or image". The quotation further says, 'The use of mass media is to foster education, science and culture... Regarded from this angle, the mass media fall into the same general category as the libraries and museums.... That of serving agencies for man's higher activities.'

The definitions and the statements given below reveal the scope, purpose and the meaning of Mass Media.

(a) The Oxford English Dictionary. 2nd ed. (1989) says " A medium of communication (such as radio, television, newspapers etc.,) that reaches a large number of people".

(b) The Random House Dictionary of the English Language, 2nd.ed. (1983) defines: "Any of the means of communication such as television or newspapers that reach very large number of people".

(c) Longman Dictionary of Mass Media & Communication edited by T.D. Connors, New York, Longman (1982) states, "print or broadcast outlet through which material is communicated in the public at large, usually means newspapers, television, radio etc."

(d) A dictionary of Media Terms edited by Edmund Penny, New York, G.P. Putnam's sons (1984) puts it: " The particular communication form used in presenting the written material, radio, T V, cable, cassette, film, live performance, holography, audio recording or whatever medium or media are chosen."

Mass media is a new social institution concerned with the production and distribution of information/knowledge in the widest sense of the word. It has a number of salient characteristics including:

1. The use of relatively advanced technology for the mass production and dissemination of information,
2. The systematic organisation and social regulation of this work and
3. The direction of information at large audiences who are unknown to the sender.

The importance of mass media is that it is a communication from one to many. Mass media increases the space the linguistic act can cover and decreases time that it takes to transmit. The medias have brought speed, ubiquity and pervasiveness to the traditional role of communication.

## STRUCTURE OF MASS MEDIA

The structure of mass media comprises four elements viz., (1) communicator, (2) Medium, (3) Message, and (4)

Audience. Wilbur Schramm has shown the structure of mass media by a diagram.

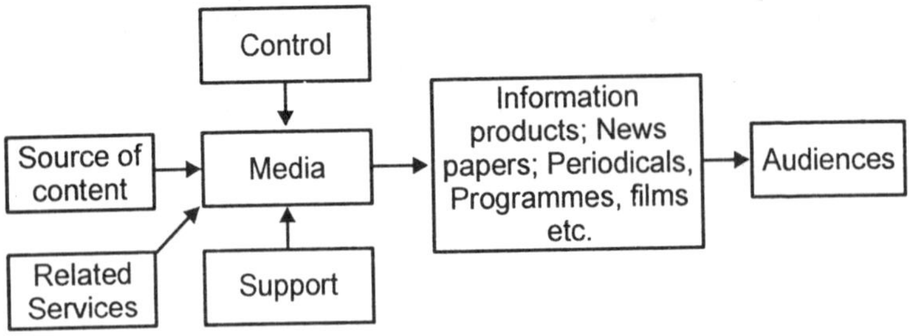


**Fig. 1. The Structure of Mass Media**

[***Source:*** Wilbur Schramm: Men, Messages and Media : A Look at Human communication. New York: Harper & Row, 1973. p.144].

## TYPES OF MASS MEDIA

Mass Media is a blend of traditional print media on the one hand and modern audiovisual media including satellite communication on the other. The following forms of communication comprise the Mass Media at present.

— Newspapers
— Radio
— Cinema
— Television and
— Video.

### Newspapers

Newspaper, a medium of mass communication usually published daily or weekly by which nascent information on current affairs, opinion and entertaining features are circulated among the people. It differs from other mass media such as radio, cinema and television since it presents its message as reading matter on paper.

Newspapers of large circulation only come under mass media but not all. They should attempt to publish a complete and balanced presentation of local, regional, national and international news. In the modern age when the medium is said to be the message, a newspaper must attempt to present its news as effectively and as attractively as possible. Page layouts, photographs, charts, type graphics etc. must help the reader to the important news. A newspaper should cover in its news both government and non-government agencies. It should have objectivity and accuracy in its reporting and audience satisfaction and profitability. Newspaper is the oldest of the mass media. News papers of some sort were there from the times of the Roman Empire. The invention of the movable type by Johann Gutenberg in Germany gave tremendous boost to this medium of communication. It is also linked to the emergence to power of the bourgeos class in Europe. It served their culturals, political and commercial activities.

Germans were the early pioneers in the production of newspapers. In the half century following the introduction of printing in 1454 A.D. a few irregular news sheets started appearing in Nurunberg, Augswengol and Cologne. The earliest one was *Newe Zeytung* dated 1502. In 1588, the *Cologne Gallo Belgicus* appeared and in 1597, *Historische Relatio* was printed. The first daily newspaper was started in Leipzig in 1660 followed by the *Jenaische Zeitung* in 1674. During the period 1500-1800 a large number of newspapers appeared throughout the Europe.

The earliest newspaper in the English language printed in England is, *Cornate*, or news from Italy, Germany, Hungarie, Spaine, and France in the year 1621. This was followed by the *Oxford Gazette* in 1665 which later moved to London and became the *London Gazette*. The first English daily, the *Daily Courant* appeared on March 11, 1702. There are many newspapers in English language which have large circulation. To name a few: *Daily Mirror*, *Daily Express*, Times, *Daily Mail*, *Herald*, *Tribune*, *New York Times*, etc. It is estimated that there are around 50,000 newspapers of all types in the world.

The story of newspapers in India is altogether a different

one. Printing presses were first brought into India in the 16th century by the Jesuit fathers for publishing evangelical literature. These were started in Goa, Madras and Calcutta. The first printed newspaper, the weekly *Bengal Gazette or Calcutta General Advertiser* was started on 29th January 1780 by James Augustus Hicky. This was also popularly known as Hicky's journal. The *Dig-Darshan, Samachar Darpan and Friend of India* appeared subsequently. The first daily newspaper published in India was The *Bengal Hurkaru* from 30th June 1836 under the editorship of James Sutherland.

Indian Press includes 41 centenarians. The Gujarat daily, *Bombay Samachar* is the oldest existing newspaper which was started in 1822. At the end of 1993, the total number of newspapers was 33,612 out of which 3740 were dailies, 275 tribi-weeklies, 11,136 weeklies and 18,461 other periodicals.

Total circulation of newspapers at the end of December 1993 was 67,611,000 copies. According to the circulation statistics, 153 are big newspapers having circulation of more than 75,000 copies, 421 are medium category with circulation of 25,000 and 75,000 copies. *Ananda Bazar Patrika, Times of India and Hindustan Times* are in the first, second and third positions circulation wise.

Newspaper is a powerful medium in India from the days of freedom struggle. In the following table the number of newspapers as in 1993 according to their language and periodicity can be seen, (see The Table in Appendix -1).

## Radio

Radio communication is one of the electronic media. In the case of newspaper, people have to be literate to use it, whereas in the case of Radio communication people even without literacy can use it and its great advantage is that too many people could listen to it. The production of radio sets is cheap and their operation easy. Through radio, people can have access to information from all countries in the world.

Radio enables the broadcast of all languages, dialects and accounts. Shortwave broadcasting added to the range of radio stations and to their political potential. Radio communication has become an important means of disseminating news and propaganda and also of education and entertainment.

The beginnings and the spread of radio communication in the west and India are interesting to know. Theoretically, radio was invented in the 1860s by James Maxwell, a Scottish physicist, who worked out the formulas of the existence of electro magnetic waves. However the first to create what we now call radio waves was the German physicist Heinrich Hertz. Subsequently there were many early experimental audio transmissions before the regular commercial radio broadcasting came into vogue.

Radio developed differently in Europe and North America. In the USA the radio broadcasting was first used with the Harding - Cox presidential election returns on November 2, 1920. The BBC (The British Broadcasting Corporation) began in 1922. It was created as a public service with appreciable independence from government. Political leaders began to use the radio broadcasting increasingly in the 1930s and 1940s. The development of tape recording in the 1950s brought new techniques and flexibility to radio. After the 1950s radio began to be found in the west in every house, in cars and in work places. People began to use a wide range of radio stations for listening programmes of their interest. The BBC and the Voice of America (VOA) are the best examples of radio broadcasting to day bringing the latest information to every home.

Radio broadcasting started in India in 1927 by private companies in Bombay and Calcutta. The Government took over the transmitters in 1930 and started operating them under the name of Indian Broadcasting Service. It was changed to All India Radio (AIR) in 1937 and it came to be known as *Akashavani* since 1957.

AIR's network comprises 179 broadcasting centres consisting of 172 full-fledged stations, three relay centres, one auxiliary centre and three exclusive *Vividh Bharati* commercial centres. There are 146 MW transmitters 50 short-wave transmission and 89 FM transmitters. The present national coverage is 89.7 per cent by area and 97.1 per cent by population. AIR is servicing as an effective medium to inform and educate people besides providing wholesome entertainment.

## Cinema

Cinema in its communication combines sound, speech and vision. It is one of the powerful genres of the electronic media. Its influence on the mass is phenomenal. It is a great entertainer.

The origins of the cinema might be traced back to 1896 when Thomas Alva Edison's vita scope was the novelty of New York and Paul's theatreograph was drawing the crowds to the London music halls. From the 1920s onwards the cinema used music incorporated in the sound track. Prior to this it was the era of silent film. The *Jazz singer* of 1928 was the first cinema with dialogue sequence. The 'talkies' became popular within no time. After the 1930s the silent cinema became obsolete. The cinema became an agency of mass communication with influence in politics, attitudes, fashion, the arts, music and language. There are cinemas of different kinds. There are cinemas for children, horrors, tragedies, comedies etc. They bring different culture, languages etc., to the notice of others.

Cinema was produced in India for the first time in 1912. R.G. Torney along with N.G. Chitre made the first film entitled, *Pundalik* in 1912. D.G. Phalke (1870-1944) produced *Raja Harichandra* in 1931. The era of silent movies was overtaken by the talkies in 1931 when Ardeshir Irani (1886-1969) produced *Alam Ara*, the first talkie cinema.

India tops the world in film production. Huge capital to

the tune of around 500 crore is invested. The cinema industry is mainly concentrated in Mumbai, Kolkata and Chennai. Nearly two lakhs people are employed in the cinema industry. The country has more than 6,000 permanent and around 4,000 touring cinema houses, The total seating capacity in these cinema houses is a little over 50 lakh, the average daily attendance of people going to cinema houses is around one crore. Indian films are exported to nearly 100 countries in the world.

Government of India had set up different organisations such as the Central Board of Certification, Films Division, National Film Development Corporation, Directorate of Film Festivals and National Film Archives for the development of the cinema industry.

The Indian cinema has tremendous impact on society and politics. Cinema writers and stars have been entering into active politics.

**Television**

Television is the most effective means of mass media known to mankind. After about 80 years of development, television made it possible for millions of people to share a single experience. With teletext, teleconferences on television, the world has become too small for communication purposes. Television is a tremendous force for political persuasion, for education and enculturation and or commercial advertisement. As on today almost all the nations in the world have privately, publicly or governmentally owned television. Television is used both by the educated and illiterates since it is a audio-visual medium.

In the 1920s and 1930s the potential of television was not widely appreciated; radio and cinema were at that time fast developing and popular means of mass communication and entertainment. Charles Frances Jenkins and John Logie Baird made experimental demonstrations of television in 1920 and

1926 respectively. However, J.G. Baird had broadcast in 1928 television pictures in colour, outdoor scenes and stereoscopic scenes.

The first regular public television system in the world began in Berlin in March 1935, its object being 'to imprint the image of Fuhrer in the hearts of the German people'. In 1936 the Olympic Games were televised. Television was converted into an electronic system in 1938. The first regular television service was inaugurated at Alexandra Palace by the British Broadcasting Corporation in November 1936. Radar and Satellite technologies contributed greatly to the development of television communication. Television has become a world-wide phenomenon today.

Doordarshan, the Indian National Television Network, is one of the largest broadcasting organisations in the world. An experimental television service was introduced in India with the starting of the Delhi Kendra with the UNESCO grant on September 15, 1959. It was extended to Mumbai city in 1972. Till 1975 only seven cities were covered by television. Now more than 85 per cent of the 1000 million population of India can receive Doordarshan programmes through a network of more than 700 terrestrial transmitters.

In the year 1982 a regular satellite link was established between Delhi and other transmitters. Doordarshan also introduced colour transmission. Doordarshan has a three-tier primary programme service - the national, the regional and the local. There is the SITE project of the Doordarshan covering 2400 backward villages in the states of Andhra Pradesh, Karnataka, Orissa, Madhya Pradesh and Rajasthan. Doordarshan broadcasts are educational and informational programmes besides entertainment and sports programmes. In 1984 a second channel was added in Delhi which was extended later to Mumbai, Kolkata and Chennai. This service known as DD2 Metro Entertainment channel has been extended to many more cities and now over 75 million people can receive programmes on this channel. Doordarshan has also entered into an agreement with the Cable News Network (CNN) and a 24-hour news and current affairs show is also available for viewers in the country. The Star TV, SITI cable, ETV etc., are also available for the viewers on different channels.

### Video

Video communication is the latest audio-visual electronic media. By the late 1970s video tapes, video recording and playing apparatus were vigorously marketed. The portable video cameras have changed the making, the cost, the production, the speed and the presentation of programmes. The distinction between video recording, television and cinema of late had become blurred. Video provides freedom to the viewer to select his programmes as per his needs. These programmes could be music, poetry, songs, lessons or any other privately recorded materials. Video parlors have become a common sight in every country. CD-ROM and multimedia is the development of video technology.

## FUNCTIONS OF MASS MEDIA

Experts assessing the influence of mass media emphasise what people learn from the media has cognitive effects in the widest sense. People may learn from the media what is normal or approved, what is right or wrong, what to expect as an individual, group or class and how they should view other groups or other nations. Aside from the nature, and magnitude of mass media effects on people, it is impossible to doubt the enormous dependence of individuals, institutions and society as a whole on mass media for a wide range of information and cultural services.

It is widely believed that mass media has an important role to play in achieving national goals. The Mc Bride Report of the UNESCO lists out the following eight functions of mass media. They are:

— dissemination of information
— socialization
— motivation
— promoting debates and discussions on public issues
— education
— cultural promotion
— entertainment
— integration

**Dissemination of Information**

Mass media made the world a global village. Through them it has become easy to know what is happening anywhere in the world. By the growth of mass media in this century, millions of people have come to know new ideas, philosophies, approaches and attitudes to life. It has brought a new dimension in man's horizon. Mass media is disseminating facts, transmitting knowledge of many things and providing the speediest and the most effective means where by leaders can approach the people in times of crises and strains. The information which is brought by the mass media is the nascent and upto date and current micro-information. The press, the radio and the television through their own agencies bring the information speedily to the doorstep of the people.

The newspapers in India publish information on Government policies, programmes and activities. They obtain information from Press Information Bureau, National Press Centre, PTI, UNI and Non-Aligned News Agencies Pool, Doordarshan and Akashavani bring out many news bulletins on political news, government programmes, weather etc.

**Socialization**

The process, of socialisation is closely linked up with the growth of mass media. The newspapers and other electronic media are powerful tools of social change. They undermine traditional values and social controls. They work for the furtherance of dominant social order at the cost of local and regional systems and cultures. The media brings people together to discuss and debate various social problems which are effecting the different sections of people in the society. By such discussions social movements get strengthened and people are persuaded to change their deviant or unconventional behaviour. Media has played a great role in creating awareness among people about untouchability, superstitions, women problems etc. The constant flow of messages from the mass media cultivates a 'mainstream' set of outlooks, assumptions and beliefs about society. People also look towards the media for ideas, information and impressions. The attitudes of people, their habits and customs gradually undergo changes because of constant and consistent messages of the mass media about social morality and social responsibilities. Cinema and television have extraordinary effect on man-woman relations, marriages, size of families and life style of people.

## Motivation

Modern societies are media dependent. Their growth and development is closely related with the mass media. They make use of media for achieving a great many goals that were handled differently in traditional society. Mass media as disseminators of information in different sectors motivate people to seek latest information or skills, needed for development Newspapers and electronic media bring the latest developments in science, technology, agriculture, medicine etc. to the notice of people even in the remotest areas and motivate them to use the fruits, of the latest innovations for the personal and social benefit. The radio and T. V. programmes on agriculture showing the use of improved variety of seeds, use of fertilisers to protect the crops can easily motivate farmers to use them. The various literary programmes can stimulate people to go to libraries and read further. The educational programmes on radio and T.V. are a boon to the student community to become motivated and learn. The audio-visual element of the programmes have greater effect on the people than the print media.

**Promoting Debates and Discussions on Public Issues**

Mass media is a vehicle for effective politics and politics is mainly dependent on mass media. The Newspapers, Radio, T.V. and Video have terrific effect on public issues. There are no societal matters which are not covered in media. The Newspapers and the Electronic media bring all the latest developments in global and national politics to the notice of people. Public matters are hotly discussed and debated on T.V., Radio and Newspapers. Mass media is extensively used for elections. Literary debates, discussions on social issues like prohibition, prostitution, corruption, pollution have become the focus of the media. The media serve as watchdog over our society and Journalists believe they have a special responsibility to critically examine the performance of the government and its organs.

The media are often criticized, however, for bias and lack of credibility. Differential exposure to media results in differential levels of knowledge, leading to structured inequalities in the, distribution of information in society. Those sectors of population which are relatively less exposed to mass media become functionally more ignorant. In democracies, this is thought to lead either to dangerous populism or to low levels of participation and to elite domination. Media is also misused by political control.

**Education**

Mass Media bring knowledge to masses. It has a captive influence on audience. It can help to equalise educational chances, especially by reaching to those who are denied chances of adequate childhood participation in education. The traditional forms of education which are associated with book work have become unexciting and dull to young people due to development of video games, film cassettes etc. Educational institutions, therefore, are now utilising film, radio, television and video as part of the instructive process. According to McLuhan, this will eventually produce hybridised cultural forms that are both entertaining and educational.

Mass media directly and indirectly help the educational process. National Policy of Education (NPE) 1986 emphasised the role of media and educational technology in the promotion of education. It stressed that media should facilitate reaching out to the most distant areas and most deprived sections of student community. AIR has a long legacy of allocation of time for educational broadcasting - both formal as well as non-formal types. THe Educational Television programmes were started in 1960 on experimental basis but they became regular from 1961 onwards. The Satellite Instructional Television Experiment (SITE) is a land mark in educational television in India. The countrywide programme of the ETV is a remarkable example of the use of media for education. Since 1984, Indian television has broadcast 11.5 hours of programmes every week for higher education: Fourteen Educational Media Research Centres and Audio Visual Research Centres have been set up by the UGC in the country for programmes production.

**Cultural Promotion**

Mass media in every country largely remained national in character. Since the media has to cater to the tastes and values of the people. The cultural forms of the country are largely reflected in the programmes of the media. The literature, poetry, drama, music, folk art, classical art and dances implode through the mass media to reach to the audience. Every one loves the past of his country. Events of history, monuments, great people of the country, form part of the programmes of the mass media.

Mass media are the cultural ambassadors of a country. When we see programmes on BBC we understand, their language, their habits, their dress and life style. The Indian epics, *Ramayan* and *Mahabarat* when they were telecast on the

Doordarshan, they depict the cultural heritage of India and make people from other cultures to understand the Indian culture. Young children can easily absorb the cultural past of a country, if the media both print and electronic ones, design programmes depicting the cultural values of the country instead of crude programmes of violence and crime. Great cinemas through their story, song, music and dances stimulate people to absorb and retain cultural values as assets of the people and their civilisation.

**Entertainment**

Mass media provide both information and entertainment. Their programmes are designed to serve the entertainment function, It reflects largely the mass tastes and mass values. When a mass medium ceases to do this, it ceases to be a mass medium.Television is the number one entertainment medium but cinema and radio are not far behind. Some of the movies were and are great hits as entertainers. T.V., Radio and Videos are common sight these days even among the middle class families. Colour is an added attraction in T.V. and cinemas. Music, songs, dances are amply used in T.V, cinemas and Radio programmes.

Even newspapers and magazines succeed or fail largely in terms of their entertainment content and quality. They intermix their information content with a dose of fun and games. However the least entertaining of the mass media is undoubtedly the newspaper. Mere entertainment is considered by many as a waste and a degradation of media potential. Many a time it is difficult to distinguish between a good entertainment and a bad entertainment. The media however, cater to the public tastes but they also help to mould public tastes and values.

Entertainment is by far the largest service of the mass media. This is especially true from the viewpoint of the audience. Television is the number one entertainment medium but cinema and radio are not far behind. Some of the movies were great hits as entertainers.

**Integration**

The idea of nation-building through the mass media has been evolving through decades. The creation of national consciousness is a major problem in a country as diverse as India with its many languages, sub-cultural traditions and ethnic groups. One of the ways of achieving national integration is by presenting through the mass media the literature, drama and music of each region to all other regions. This helps the different sections of people of the country to understand the cultures, habits, customs, festivals and life styles of each other.

The vast power of mass media has implications to democracy. The media moulds the people to things of one nation and one people under the democratic set up. Through their programmes they impress the people to get united against external threats and internal disturbances. Newspapers through their columns project the common problems which the country is facing and thus make peoples to discuss and debate the common problems of the country in a national perspective instead of regional Jingoism. Through mass media, we find, the literature, poetry, stories etc are translated to the benefit of the people of other regions.

## LIBRARIES AND MASS MEDIA

Libraries are social institutions. They are established by mandate for providing access to information to all sections of people irrespective of their class, colour, race, caste and sex. They have to provide information free to all without collecting any fee. Libraries have been in existence from ancient times. They have started growing enormously after the invention of printing. They have become indispensable source for the furtherance of education. Libraries, through dissemination of information, have caused the emergence of democratic ideas of freedom and equality. Different kinds of libraries like public libraries, academic libraries, special libraries, industrial libraries, private libraries are in vogue. Libraries have become catalysts of social change and development.

Mass media is a recent phenomenon when compared with libraries. Cinema, Radio and T.V. have come to pubic use only in the first quarter of the last century. Though the Newspapers were in existence for the last 150 years, their circulation earlier was limited; Newspapers with large circulation is a phenomenon of the 20th century only. Mass media provide both information and entertainment. They provide the latest, upto date and pinpointed information to the public. The information provided by the mass media is uniform, fast and reach even the remotest areas where libraries are not available.

Today the concept of library comprises many media besides books. An enlightened policy on library must take into account the possibilities of all media. Educational concerns must be extended to the whole of the media. If tapes are better than books for learning languages or any subject, look after them.

Libraries and mass media are two different channels of information and their similarities and dissimilarities are detailed below:

1. Libraries are generally used by people who are literate. Illiterates who cannot read and write normally keep away from libraries. Whereas the mass media with the exception of newspapers are listened and viewed by all.
2. The actual users of libraries are few of the total population whereas films, radio, T.Vs are used by more people.
3. The readers have to go to the libraries to use their collection by the people whereas the mass media is available at home. People can use them easily according

to the convenience of their leisure.

4. The library facilities can be used singly by individuals, whereas mass media can be used simultaneously by the entire family.

5. The purpose of the libraries is to provide information and knowledge whereas the purpose of mass media is largely entertainment. Films, radios, T.V. and even newspapers contain information mainly designed to fill the leisure time but not for serious purpose.

6. Access to public libraries is free. Anybody without any restrictions of class, caste, race, sex , rich and poor can have free access to the libraries whereas for mass media one has to spend money. People have to subscribe to newspapers and purchase the radio and TV to hear and view them. They are expensive and poorer people can least afford.

7. Libraries provide reference service, information service and borrowing facilities, where as the mass media programmes can be viewed and listened at the slotted time schedules only., except in the case of the use of a video.

8. Libraries are essential for education. Mass media are also used for educational purposes. Radio and T.V. are used for broadcasting educational programmes for students in schools and colleges. ETV is largely utilised by the open universities where the education is imparted by the distance mode.

9. Variety of programmes and news are brought to the people instantly by the mass media. Whereas it is not possible for the libraries to be instantaneous in bringing the global news and information to the people like the mass media.

10. Libraries are cultural institutions which preserve the

culture of the people in the documents and transmit them to the posterity. Whereas the programmes of the mass media are time bound.

11. Mass media are largely part of the libraries these days. They cannot replace the libraries. They are at best supplements and complements to the libraries. News papers, radio, T.V. and video films are largely used in the libraries. Video books and films are common sight in the libraries of the advanced countries They can be borrowed like other documents from the libraries.
12. There is general criticism that mass media because of their attraction may mislead people to populism, voilence, crime etc., Libraries are centres of peace and harmony.

## CONCLUSION

Both libraries and mass media provide information to their readers, listeners and viewers. The information available in the libraries is in the form of books, periodicals and other documents. This is mostly print media at present. This information could be utilised only by the literates, whereas the information through Radio, T.V. and cinema even illiterates can obtain by listening and viewing them. Information provision through audio-visual media is direct, fast and reaches all people uniformly.

Libraries and Mass Media are essential for social development. Mass Media reaches to the places where libraries have not developed or available. Newspapers, Radio, T.V. and Cinema bring out latest information though their different types of programmes. Their information is topical and pinpointed. Their influence on people is phenomenal. Though there is criticism regarding the ill effects of T.V. and cinema, on children and students, still these media could be used effectively to develop interest and motivation for developmental activities.

Mass media can create interest and quest in people for further information. Libraries are the ultimate sources of information. Potential readers can be turned into regular readers by libraries reaching out to the people through their services. Hence mass media can supplement and complement the libraries but cannot replace them. Library materials are available on regular basis to borrow, whereas the Radio scripts, and T.V. programmes are not easily available after their slotted time for use.

## REFERENCES


1. ACHARYA, R.N. *Television in India.* Delhi ; Manas Publications, 1987.
2. BENGE, Ronald C. *Libraries and Cultural Change.* London: Clive Bingley, 1970.
3. CABECEIRAS, James. *The Multimedia Library: Materials Selection Use.* New York: Academic Press, 1978.
4. CHALAPATHI RAU, M. *The press.* New Delhi : NBT, 1974.
5. CHATTERJI, P.C. *Broadcasting in India.* New Delhi: Sage Publications, 1987.
6. DOVE, Jack. *The Audio-Visual. The availability and exploitation of non-print materials with special reference to libraries.* London: Andre Deutsch, 1975.
7. HARRISON, Helen P. *Film library techniques.* London: Focal Press, 1973.
8. HILLARD, Robert L. *Radio Broadcasting: An introduction to Sound Medium* 3rd. ed. New York : Longman, 1985.
9. INDIA. Ministry of Information and Broadcasting. *Mass Media in India - 1978.* New Delhi : Publications Division, 1978.
10. INDIA. Ministry of information and Broadcasting. *Mass Media in India - 1993.* New Delhi: Publication Division, 1994.
11. Mc BRIDE, Seam et.al. *Many voices, one world.* London: Kogan page, 1980.
12. Me LUHAN, Marshall. *Understanding Media: The Extensions of Man.* New York : Me Graw Hill, 1964.

13. SARKAR, R.C.S. *The press in India.* New Delhi: S.Chand & Co, 1980.

14. SCHRAMM, Wilber (ed) *Mass Communications: A Book of selected Readings.* 2nd. ed. Urbana : University of Illinois Press, 1975.

15. SCHRAMM, Wiiber. Men, *Messages and Media: A Look at Human Communication.* New York : Harper & Row, 1973.

# APPENDIX - 1

## *Table 1. Number of Newspapers in 1993 According to Ixingitage & Periodicals*

| *Lang-uage* | *Dailies* | *Tri/bi weeklies* | *Weeklies* | *Fortnight-lies* | *Month-lies* | *Quarter-lies* | *Bi-month Half-yearlies* | *Annuals* | *Total* |
|---|---|---|---|---|---|---|---|---|---|
| *English* | 256 | 18 | 637 | 496 | 216 | 1025 | 590 | 133 | 5316 |
| *Hindi* | 1674 | 107 | 6050 | 2012 | 2230 | 381 | 120 | 22 | 12596 |
| *Assamese* | 10 | 3 | 51 | 29 | 41 | 10 | 9 | 1 | 154 |
| *Bengali* | 80 | 11 | 503 | 376 | 582 | 360 | 116 | 8 | 2036 |
| *Gujarati* | 78 | 7 | 289 | 120 | 387 | 47 | 36 | 10 | 974 |
| *Kannada* | 203 | 5 | 289 | 120 | 387 | 47 | 36 | 10 | 974 |
| *Kashmiri* | 0 | 0 | 1 | 0 | 0 | 0 | 0 | 0 | 1 |
| *Konkani* | 0 | 0 | 2 | 1 | 1 | 0 | 0 | 0 | 4 |
| *Malayalam* | 184 | 2 | 154 | 137 | 585 | 42 | 17 | 8 | 1129 |
| *Manipuri* | 10 | 0 | 3 | 5 | 3 | 3 | 2 | 0 | 26 |
| *Marathi* | 225 | 17 | 579 | 140 | 397 | 87 | 34 | 82 | 1561 |
| *Nepali* | 1 | 2 | 12 | 5 | 7 | 16 | 5 | 0 | 48 |
| *Oriya* | 46 | 2 | 84 | 57 | 224 | 73 | 18 | 4 | 508 |
| *Punjabi* | 79 | 15 | 296 | 63 | 204 | 25 | 17 | 1 | 700 |
| *Sanskrit* | 3 | 0 | 6 | 2 | 13 | 13 | 4 | 0 | 41 |
| *Sindhi* | 8 | 0 | 31 | 9 | 32 | 6 | 2 | 0 | 88 |
| *Tamil* | 297 | 34 | 324 | 193 | 578 | 23 | 9 | 2 | 1460 |
| *Telugu* | 87 | 2 | 206 | 138 | 226 | 20 | 6 | 1 | 796 |
| *Urdu* | 389 | 18 | 1022 | 297 | 437 | 44 | 14 | 3 | 2224 |
| *Bilingual* | 47 | 17 | 445 | 255 | 930 | 277 | 106 | 27 | 2104 |
| *Multilinguals* | 13 | 4 | 77 | 41 | 190 | 59 | 25 | 7 | 416 |
| *Others* | 50 | 11 | 75 | 22 | 104 | 44 | 8 | 0 | 314 |
| | 3,740 | 275 | 11,136 | 4,571 | 9,837 | 2,589 | 1,153 | 311 | 33,612 |

(***Source:*** *India 1995 A reference Annual*. New Delhi, Publication Division, 1996. p.278.)

# 4

# Automation, Networking and Consortia : An Indian Developmental Perspective

## INTRODUCTION

Information and its twin derivatives knowledge and wisdom are God's gift to *Homo Sapiens*. Information flowing between the two banks, times past and times present, created cultures and civilizations which are the proud witness of the human Journey throughout history. Information, as the life blood of human beings, is harboured in libraries for human good. Hence the libraries and the librarianship are the continuous interplay between social needs and technological innovations through the centuries. The turbulency of information inflow increased century after century. Now the flow is doubling every five to six years.

Many attempts were made in the medieval times to control the chaotic conditions of the turbulency of information flow. Gutenberg's discovery of Print, Konrad Gesner's Universal Bibliography, Universal Encyclopedias, IFLA's UPA Programme were such attempts. These were not able to provide the required facility of "all information to all people".

## TECHNOLOGY

Many revolutionary shifts have taken place in technology and telecommunication. Charles Babbage and Herman Hollerith discovered and developed respectively, a machine called computer which later has become both fascinating and intimidating. The Computer was primarily for doing arithmetic in the beginning. It began to be used for different purposes in the mid 1940s. Many communication scientists such as Colin Cherry, Shanon, Weaver, Weiner, Ackoff, Yovits revolutionized the communication system. The combination of computers and communication pushed the Information Technology and the internet to the fore front to solve the problems of information, control, retrieval and supply.

## COMPUTERS AND LIBRARIES

Computers began to be used for library operations and services from the year 1954. The USA was the first country to use the computers in libraries. This was followed by the UK and the other developed western countries. The Library of Congress began to bring out the MARC from 1961 which was the landmark in automation of library operations.

In the evolution of library automation there are three phases in development. The first phase of development was from 1954 to 1970. The second one was from 1970 to 1990. The Third phase is from 1990 till today. The three phases synchronize with the five generations of computer development. The concept of computerization in India started in the Second Phase. The advantages of Library Automation may be considered before we deal with the introduction of library automation in India.

## ADVANTAGES OF AUTOMATION IN LIBRARIES

- Library automation enables to create and maintain large

bibliographic databases which were not there earlier. Earlier attempts to have Universal Bibliographic Control by Konard Gesner, Paul Otlet and La Fontaine and Encyclopaedists failed miserably.

- The automation provides consistency and accuracy in the context of databases.
- Automation provided international standards like the Dublin Core for bibliographic description.
- Library automation provides speedy access, removing the barriers of space and time, to information and documents at global level.
- Library automation through various techniques such as search engines, networking and the internet saves the precious time of the user community.
- Library automation is a research facilitator and promoter through web technology.

## EARLY STAGES OF AUTOMATION IN INDIA

The automation of library activities in the L.C. and the British Library with MARC and BLASE and JANET respectively have become a pacesetter and precursor to many other countries in the world to follow suite. GOI felt the need for automation and networking of its libraries in the 1980s. During the 7th plan period the Department of Electronics Projected ambitious programmes for the development of networks such as the NICNET, INDONET, RAILNET, OILNET and BANKNET. The NIC Commissioned the NICNET in 1977. During the 7th Plan period (1985-1990) the planning commission appointed a Working Group under the Chairmanship of Dr. N. Sheshagiri on libraries and Informatics. The Committee had submitted its report in July 1984 under the title "*Modernisation of Library Services and Informatics*". The Report is in 9 Chapters containing 95 pages. It was ably prepared for the modernization and computerization of all types of libraries in the country. It is a land mark report in the country for automation of libraries.

The Seshagiri Report identified some Libraries and Organizations which were already using computers for their library and information activities. They are:

— Bhabha Atomic Research Centre (BARC) Mumbai.

— Tata Institute of Fundamental Research (TIFR) Mumbai.

— National Informatics Centre (NIC) New Delhi.

— Documentation Research Training Centre (DRTC) Bangalore.

— Indian National Science Documentation Centre (INSDOC) New Delhi.

— Indian Institute of Technology (IIT) Chennai.

— Bharat Heavy Electrical Ltd. (BHEL) Hyderabad.

The highlights of the computerization activities since 1964 are as follows:

1964 - INSDOC and IIT, Kanpur made efforts to bring out a National Union Catalogue of Scientific Serials using IBM,/ 1620 Computer.

1968/69- INSDOCs has started efforts for use of Computers to the development of information production. The use of IBM/1620 for the preparation of a 'Roaster of Technical Translators in India' and the Author and Subject Index for the ISA at the Delhi University.

1970- BARC Started Participating in INIS. TIFR started to prepare library catalogues. DRTC began DOCFINDER.

1976- I.I.T. Chennai and INSDOC started the CHEM/SDI Information Retrieval System.

1977- DRTC developed a SDI Service for the BHEL, Hyderabad.

1978- Electronics Commission began to use HP21 MX Mini Computer System.

1980/81- Physical Research Laboratory, Ahmedabad developed Computerised Periodicals Management System and Book Procurement System. NIC developed an integrated online Bibliographical Database.

1983- NICNET started for accessing the NIC's Library Database.

1984- A Computer terminal installed at NIC Library for information retrieval Jobs. NIC also prepared a Pilot Project to the National Medical Library and a Legal Information Retrieval System for the Ministry of Law, New Delhi.

## NISSAT

In 1985 the NISSAT convened a meeting under the Chairmanship of the Director-General, CSIR. Among many other things one of the recommendations of this meeting was the establishment of a science and technology library in Kolkata and the promotion of automation and networking in the city. The CMC Ltd was commissioned to prepare a feasibility report which was published in 1989. In the meanwhile, the India International Centre approached the NISSAT in 1988 to start a network project which was later in 1992, registered as DELNET under the societies of Registration Act, 1960.

## CALIBNET

It is a network of 40 libraries in the city of Kolkata. It was wholly funded by the NISSAT. It uses software called 'MAITRAYEE' developed by the CMC Ltd based on the software INGRESS 502. CALIBNET has not so far created any Union Catalogue of books in the 40 libraries in the city of Kolkata. It is offering only CD-ROM database searching facility. It has not yet created of its own. Its help to the libraries in the city of Kolkata is limited.

## DELNET

DELNET covers 67 libraries in Delhi. It uses a software called DELSIS' which was based on 'BASIS PLUS'. It provides INTERNET access and E-mail facilities to its members.

DELNET has a Union catalogue of 1068 lakhs books and a Union list of periodicals of 116 Libraries. It has developed a Database of periodical articles. It may be considered that the DELNET through its facilities created under the leadership of Dr. H.K. Kaul may be considered as the first library network in India. DELNET has also arranged several training programmes for its participating libraries.

In the subsequent years other networks such as MALIBNET (Chennai); BONET (Mumbai), Mylibnet (Mysore), BALNET (Bangalore), ADINET (Ahmedabad), and PUNENET (Pune) had emerged with the support of the NISSAT. Besides the networks, the NISSAT had done commendable work in automation and in establishing sectoral information centres in specialized fields. They are NICLA (CLRI Chennai), NICFOS (CFTRI, Mysore), NICMAP(CMTR, Banglore) NICDAP (CDRL Lucknow) NICTAS (ATIRA. Ahmedabad) NICHEM (NCL, Pune) NICACA (CGCRI, Kolkata) NCB (INSDOC, New Delhi) NICRYS (UOM, Chennai) NICDRO (NAL, Bangalore) NICMAN (IIM, Ahmedabad) and NICMAS (NIO, Goa). For development of automation NISSAT had created the LISFORUM, VAPIS and CD-ROM based SDI Services in various institutions.

## OTHER INITIATIVES

Government of India and the University Grants Commission took many initiatives for the development of automation and networking in the country. They are:

1. Committee on the National Policy on Library and Information System (1988).
2. Committee on National Network System for Universities/ Libraries (1988).

3. UGC Curriculum Development Committee (1992).
4. Second UGC Curriculum Development Committee (1997).
5. National Knowledge Commission (2007).

The Committee on the National Policy on Library and Information System under the Chairmanship of D.P. Chattopadhyaya though mainly concerned with the public libraries, suggested among many other recommendations for the modernization and the introduction of Computer technology in the libraries. The recommendations of the committee have not been implemented. The UGC Committee on National Network System for University Libraries suggested for the setting up of the INFLIBNET at Ahmedabad.

The UGC also took initiative to set up a committee in 1992 under the Chairmanship of Prof. P.N. Kaula in 1992 and a second committee under the chairmanship of Prof. C.R. Karisiddappa to streamline the syllabi of the BLISC and MLISC courses in the Indian Universities Dynchornism giving with the Modern technological developments. The committees recommended the introduction of Computer Technology papers at the BLISC and MLISC levels. In the year 2007 the Government of India appointed a National Knowledge Commission under the chairmanship of Sam Petroda with prime focus on five key areas of the knowledge paradigm - access to knowledge, knowledge concepts, knowledge creation, knowledge application and development of better knowledge service. In all these five areas the IT plays a thrust role.

## INFLIBNET

It is a pet project of the UGC Chairman Prof. Yashpal. It began its operations in 1991 with its headquarters at Ahmedabad. Prof Yashpal thought that a library and Information Network of the maginitude of the INFLIBNET is very essential for the country in the modem context of computer and communication technologies. The work of the

INFLIBNET was reviewed by a Review Committee headed by Dr S. Venkateswaran in 1996.

The INFLIBNET was supposed to finance all the University Libraries to introduce Computer Technology and also to bring them under one umbrella of network interconnecting various libraries and information centres in the country and to improve the capability in information handing and services. It was to create an online union catalogue of books, periodicals and other documentary materials for the purpose of resource sharing among the participating libraries. It is a commendable project but it is moving very slowly According to the Review Committee (1996) that the INFLIBNET was able to create 50,000 records for books, 50,000 records for theses and dissertations and 30,000 records for serials. It is not able to deliver the results in the expected scale. Prof. Yashpal's dreams about the impact of the INFLIBNET have been belied.

## CONSORTIA

The lack of any single national network connecting Arunachal Pradesh to Gujarat and Kanya Kumari to Kashmir, Open access to information, document delivery and information service facilities in our country have become unsatisfactory when compared with the information infrastructure in other developed countries. India is a big and gigantic country in South-East Asia. It is booming with developmental activities. A national network uniting various parts of the country is a pre-requisition for its development and to find - proper place in the comity of nations. Some of the special organizations and institutions in order to overcome the drawbacks of lack of national network began to pool their information resources with other institutions which have similar objectives like them. They form a consortia with them as it is in practice in the Western Countries. The concept of consortia is a recent one started in 1960's. Library consortia is a static alliance of libraries with a common interest, not under the same institutional control, but usually restricted to a geographical area, number of libraries, types of materials or subjects of common interest. Consortia are established for resource sharing and to provide maximum access to their resources to the members. The advantages of a library consortium are:

— Provides the ability to share resources without loosing identity.
— Provides greater buying power and maximum access to information resources to users.
— Acquires the document materials at lower prices, particularly in the case of e-journals.
— Provides quality to library services.
— Increases the efficiency of library staff.
— Saves the time of library users and library staff.

Some of the consortia well known in the USA and UK are: WRLC (the Washington Research Library Consortium) VIVA (Virtual Library of Virginia) OHIOLINK (Ohio Library and Information Network) PALCI (Pennsylvania Academic Library, Consortium Inc) CURL (Consortium of University Research Libraries) JANET (Joint Academic Network). A number of library consortia are also functioning in India. They are:

- **FORSA (*Forum For Resource Shaving In Astronomy & Astrophysical*)**

It is a group of five libraries consortium in the filed of Astronomy and Astrophysics. It was established in 1982 with its headquarters at Bangalore. The institutions participating in this consortium are: Raman Research Institute, Indian Institute of Astrophysics, Tata Institute of Fundamental Research, Inter University Center for Astronomy and Astrophysics.

- **INDEST (*Indian National Digital Library In Science And Technology*)**

It was set up by the Ministry of Human Resources

Development (MHRD) in 2002 with its headquarters at the LIT, New Delhi. There are 38 institutions in this consortiam including IISC, IITs, NITs, RECs, IIMs and few other institutions. It has a good number of e-resources. A Natioı.al Review Committee is responsible for its over all policy and monitoring.

- **CSIR (*Council Of Science And Industrial Research*) *Consortium***

It was established in 2004 by the CSIR with its headquarters at the National Institute of Science Communication and Information Research (NISCA1R) New Delhi. It provides access to 4500 International Journals to all S & T Personnel of the CSIR.

- **HELNET (*Health Science Library And Information Network*)**

This was established in 2002 in Bangalore. The subject coverage of this consortium are health, medicine and bio-medical Science. This consortia was promoted by the Rajiv Gandhi University of Health Sciences, Bangalore.

- **IIM (*Indian Institute Of Management*)**

The six institutions of Management have formed this consortium.

- **UGC-INFONET**

This was established by the UGC. Its headquarters is at INFLIBNET, Ahmedabad. Major e-Journals are available at one point. It was launched in October, 2003.

- **IGCAR (*Indira Gandhi Centre Atomic Research*) *Consortium***

This consortium was established at Kalpakkam, Chennai - This covers 12 units and 14 field stations spread all over India. All member institutes are able to access, *Science Direct* on itah - line containing 1700e-journals.

- **J-GCC: J-Gate Cluster Content**

It has more than 4000 Journals for access at one point.

- **SNDT University**

The SNDT University in coordination with six other universities is maintaining the Library and Information Science Abstract (LISA).

- **UO HYD MATHS**

It was established by the University of Hyderabad in 1977. The other members of this consortium are the IISC and ISI. This consortium covers only Mathematics literature. Online access to full text of all resources of AMS is available. Library Consortia have emerged as a necessity for libraries due to technological advancement, availability of large amount of resources, changing user needs, declining of Library budgets. Most of the Indian Libraries showing interest either to form or join the consortia. Certain standards are essential for the consortia for their successful operation.

## SUGGESTIONS

- India is the biggest country in the South East Asia. In the geopolitics of the area it has to play a leading part. It is, therefore, has to modernize immediately its telecommunication and networks systems.
- The country has to give importance to the Library and Information Systems as it gives to educational sector. The excellence of education cannot be there without the effective and efficient information system.
- The present print and electronic media like Newspapers, Radio, and TV are not sufficient enough to cover all the inhabitations in the country. There are more than 5 lakh villages are there in the country without libraries or information access.
- The subject "Library" is in the State List of Powers. It should be immediately transferred to the 'Concurrent List" of Powers, as it was done in the case or "education" by amending the Constitution of India.

- Government of India, UGC, AICTE, RRRLF and the State Governments should ensure at least 8 to 10% of their annual budgets for establishment, development and modernization of the public libraries. Intellectuals are generated by the consumption of information and knowledge but not by the consumption of politics.
- It is high time for our politicians and planners to realise that *Kudu* (Food) *Gudda* (Cloth) and *Gudu* (Shelter) are not enough for the development of our country but *Vidhya* (education) and *Vignan* (Knowledge) are also essential.
- There should be a National Policy for Libraries. The report of D.P. Chattopadhyaya should be dusted, retrieved, energized and acted on immediately.
- There is no need to appoint more and more committees and commissions like the knowledge commission without action onthe recommendations of the earlier committees and commissions. An ounce of action is more important than tons of theory.
- This vast country needs immediately a National Network like BLAISE or JANET connecting all types of libraries, Information centres, Institutions from Arunachal Pradesh to Gujarat and from Kashmir to Kanya Kumari. The lack of it is so striking and staring on the face of all thinking people in this country. The present networks such as the INFLIBNET, CALIBNET, DELNET etc. are nothing but show pieces. The National Library of the country is languishing.
- The library professionals and intellectuals of this country have to awake and arise demanding access to information and 'All information to all people'. Democracy would die without proper infrastructure of information delivery. The advent of the Information society and knowledge society is a mirage without proper information infrastructure.

## REFERENCES

1. Behera, Sangita (2008). Library consortia in India, A study in; E-Libraries: Problems and Perspectives, edited by L.S.Ramaiah et al. New Delhi: Allied publishers.
2. Crawford, W. (1995). Future Libraries, dreams, madmen and reality. Chicago: ALA.
3. Haravu, L.J. (1993). Library automation and networks in India: an overview of recent development. *Annals of Library Science and Documentation*, 40 (1): 32-40
4. Haravu, L.J. and Siddartha, M. (2004). Some experiences in consortia development and possible lessons for India. In: Library Consortia: Seminar Papers and Proceedings, edited by N.Laxman Rao et al. Hyderabad: IATLIS: 339-349.
5. India, University Grants Commission, New Delhi (1988). Development of an Information and Library network: Report of the Inter-Agency working Group. New Delhi: UGC.
6. India, University Grants Commission (2001). UGC Model Curriculum: Library and Information Science. New Delhi, - UGC.
7. Kaul, H.K. (1999). Library resource sharing and networks. New Delhi: Virgo Publication.
8. Kushwah, Shivpal Singh, et al. (2003). Consortia initiative in Indian Libraries. International CALJBER-2003. Ahmedabad: NIRMA: 347-357.
9. Laxman Rao. N et al (2004) Library Consortia: Seminar papers & proceedings. Hyderabad: Indian Association of Teachers of Library and Information Science.
10. Mahajan. S.G. (1992). Resource sharing and networking of University libraries in India. *University News* 31st August: 79-85.
11. Majumdar, Apurba Jyoti (2008). Impact of Library consortia on LIS education In: E-Libraries: Problems and perspectives, edited by Ramaiah L.S. et al New Delhi: Allied Publishers.
12. Murthy, T.A. V. (2002). Resources sharing or consortia for India In: information management in E-Libraries. New Delhi, Allied Publishers.

13. National Knowledge Commission (2007). Libraries, Gateways to knowledge: A road map for revitalization, New Delhi: NKC.
14. Potter, U.G. (1997). Recent trends in state wide academic library consortia. *Library Trends*, 45 (3): 416-434.
15. Raj Goli, Iqbalahmad U, Birdie and Karisiddappa, C.R. (2005). Use of information resources through consortia mode in India Library and Information centres: A case study of FORSA Consortium. *IASLJC Bulletin*, 50 (2): 74-82.
16. Rama Murti (Chairman). (1990) Towards an enlightened and human society: Report of the Committee for review of National Policy on Education, 1986:- Final Report, New Delhi.
17. Seshagiri, N. (1984). Report of the working Group of the Planning Commission on modernization of Library services and informatics for the seventh five year plan, 1985-90. New Delhi: Planning Commission.
18. INDEST [http://www:library"iitb.ac.in/indest/induc.html]
19. INFLIBNET centre [http://wwwinflibnet, adin/]
20. REFLINET [http://www.rguhs.ac.in/un/abouthtml]
21. UGC Infonet [http://web.inflibnet.ac.in/info/ugeinfonet/ugc infonet.Jsp].

# 5

# Role of Raja Rammohun Roy Library Foundation in Improving Knowledge base in Rural India

## INTRODUCTION

Information like the other universal phenomena—land, sky, (light) fire, water and air—is a fundamental resource. *Homo sapiens* sans information are barbarians, information without mankind is a myth, and information is created by man and utilized by man. It is unimaginable to utilize the other resources without information resource. Mankind through its journey of a millennium or two had many paradigm shifts in their development. Information alone kept the man on the highest pedestal of civilization. The use of more and more information and for more and more purposes and more and more times made the man to bring about overall development on the earth. Today there is a dichotomy among the people as 'the information rich' and 'the information poor'. This is reflected in the uneven growth and development of the countries as well as of communities within the countries. Hence it is a proven fact that information is an important resource for the banishment of poverty, disease, illiteracy, misunderstanding and wars in the world.

The body of information in the universe has not been the creation of one person or one community or one country. It is a cumulative wealth of the mankind. It is, therefore, rightly said by Karl Popper that the mankind lives in three worlds—physical, mental, and the information world. The unlimited wealth of information is generally beyond the reach of every ordinary person among all the communities in the world. Therefore, today's slogan is that all men should have access to information at all places and at all times. Public libraries are the gateways as stated in the UNESCO-Public Library Manifesto for accessing information. Oral communication has limited reach and it is like the writ on the water. It is not sustainable information. Information received at the educational institutions is only basic one and limited in character because of the limitation of the academic programs and courses, whereas the public libraries of all kinds provide unlimited body of information for lifelong learning and education.

## PUBLIC LIBRARY SYSTEM IN INDIA

During the British rule in India, libraries were completely neglected since the authorities presumed that the libraries are the centers of sedition and breeding grounds, of revolt against their rule. Even after 62 years of India's Independence, libraries still have not grown and developed in the way as they should have been in a democratic set up. The position of academic libraries, except the school libraries, is a little better because of the UGC's efforts. The public library system was completely neglected. Education and libraries are like two eyes but the Constitution of India had done injustice in the case of public library system. Education and public libraries were originally classified in the Constitution as State Subjects. Later the Constitution was amended and the subject education was shifted into Concurrent List. It means that the Central government can act on the matter of education and allocate funds for subject areas in the Union and Concurrent Lists of powers. The State Governments which have to look after the public libraries have treated them on a very low priority. It is evident from the legislation enacted in the states for the public libraries system during the last sixty years. Out of 36 States and Union Territories around 16 States only passed library legislation and the remaining states like Assam, Madhya Pradesh, Punjab, and Jammu and Kashmir have yet to pass it for the development of public libraries. India is a sub continent with 3,336 cities and towns and 5,57,137 villages with only 49,757 villages libraries. It amounts to only 9 per cent the villages are having public libraries and the remaining 91 per cent are without village library service. Nearly 85 per cent of India's population resides in rural India, and these are the people who are involved in agricultural production. They form the backbone of the national economy as India is an agrarian state. Not only they are economically poor but also poor information wise.

The village community consists of various sections like farmers, horticulturists, labour, gold smiths, craftsmen etc. In their daily activity they require knowledge both old and new to shift themselves from less productive areas to better productive areas to meet their increasing needs. Taking an example of a farmer in a village, he would require latest information on different crops, seeds, fertilizers, pesticides, labour, weather and marketing. Without information on these areas the farmer is left high and dry. The different schemes and concessions as given by the Central and State Governments and banking institutions are not reaching to the farmers living in the remote villages as they are not aware of it. The information should reach the village folks as they are creators of wealth. The public library system should be geared to reach the unreached to provide information and knowledge.

With the advent of the computer technology, and Internet, telecommunication, networking can make information available from one corner of the world to the other within no time. The governments should seize this opportunity and make a paradigm shift in their planning and vision for taking information to all sections of people at all levels. Many reports by the committees appointed by the state and central governments stressed the importance of the information. It is a mandatory on the part of the authorities to implement their recommendations. Dr. Damie in his work entitled

**Fig. : The Hierarchical Position of the Public Library System in Vogue in the Country**

Minister In-Charge Public Libraries
↓
Library Council
↓
Directorate, Public Libraries
↓
State Central Library (Maintained by State Government)
↓
Divisional Libraries (One in each Revenue Division)
↓
Maintained by State Government
↓
Local Library Authorities
↓
District Central Library Maintained by LLA
↓
Branches of DCL in each Town
↓
Block Central Library of Rural Areas
↓
Villages Libraries as Branches of BCL
↓
Book Deposit Centers

*''Communication of Modem Ideas and Knowledge in Indian Village* stated that "the problem of communication of modern ideas to 5,57,137 villages of India is a central one. Rural roads are being built to bring into contact with the outside world. The All-India Radio has taken major programme of placing community radio sets in village centres and giving them most important programs. Yet thousands of villages are still untouched, and most of them are gradually coming into contact with the programme agencies". To quote one another such report by Archarya Rama Murthi entitled *"Towards Enlightened and Humane Society"* (1990) stated "In the backward areas including SC, ST habitats a network of linked libraries should be of bicycle borne mobile libraries or para schools based libraries should be brought under implementation. These libraries need to be enriched with creative children's literature. While the children's literature would be primarily in the regional languages, efforts should be made to increase the availability of the children's books in the local dialects or languages spoken in educationally backward areas".

## ESTABLISHMENT OF THE RRRLF

The public libraries all over India are in pathetic condition. Their progress is not at par with the progress of the educational institutions. The State Governments are not providing adequate funds for the growth and development of the public libraries in spite of the library cess imposed by some of the state governments. In order to set right the situation the Government of India has various options before it. Instead of taking the entire responsibility for the development of the public libraries, the Central Government opted for a lesser burden by creating the RRRLF. The RRRLF was created by the Central Government in 1972 on the occasion of the bicentenary of the birth of Raja Rammohun Roy for "supporting and promoting a network of libraries, which could carry books and inculcate reading habits to the remotest parts of the country". Raja Rammohun Roy was a social reformer and a founding father of the Indian Renaissance. The RRRLF was inaugurated formally on May 20, 1972 at the campus of the National Library, Belvedere, Kolkota, with a goal to ensure library facilities for all people living in both urban and rural areas. The Foundation had laid down 29 objectives for its operation. The most important ones are:

- To promote library movement in the country;
- To enunciate a national library policy and to work towards its adoption by the Central and State Governments;
- To help build up a national library system by integrating the services of National Libraries, State Central Libraries, District Libraries and other types of libraries (children's academic and special) through inter-library lending system;
- To propagate the adoption of library legislation in the country;
- To provide financial and technical assistance to libraries;
- To establish in the country Regional Library Service Centers which will offer reprographic and book preservation services to assist in the reproduction and proper preservation of reading material, whether printed or in manuscript form
- To maintain a national register of qualified librarians and their fields of specialization;
- Generally to take all such measures as may be found necessary form time to time to promote library development and its utilization in the country.

Prof. S. Nurul Hasan, the then Minister of Education, Social Welfare and Culture stressing the objectives of the RRRLF in detail at the inaugural function stated that "The primary objective of Raja Rammohun Roy Library Foundation will be to stimulate the library movement in India by enabling the various State and Central libraries to carry out their functions more effectively. The Foundation will make special efforts to ensure that new libraries are set-up in all districts where they do not exist and that district libraries are enabled to serve a chain of libraries in the rural areas so that these come within the reach of the common people. This would mean the setting-up of mobile units spread all over India, especially in rural areas. The mobile units will carry reading materials for the purpose of education, as well as for entertainment. The foundation will also pay special attention to the needs of children and the handicapped persons. In other words, it is going to launch a multi pronged movement in order to give a fillip to the dormant library service in the country".

The Government of India in order to implement and supervise the objectives stated above established a Directorate of Libraries in the Ministry of Culture. The RRRLF during the last 35 years had initiated many programmes for the establishment and development of public libraries in the country. The foundation had assisted about 35,000 public libraries all over the country during its 35 years of operations. Some of the important programmes initiated are:

- Conserted efforts to enact library legislation in States and Union Territories.
- To evolve a national public library policy.
- Survey of the conditions of the public libraries.
- Aid to establish the public libraries in the country.
- Provision of matching grants for purchasing and distribution of books directly by the RRRLF to the public libraries in the country.
- Aid for the construction of buildings and purchasing furniture and other requisites.
- Modernization of public libraries by applying IT and automation.
- Pursuing the DPLs to open separate sections for women

and children, physically handicapped, blind etc.,

- Arranging annual lectures on public libraries in various parts of the country.
- Assisting the Library Associations, LIS Departments, and NGO's to conduct conferences, seminars, workshops etc.,
- Announcing the best libraries awards.
- Training and retraining the library personnel working in public libraries.
- Encouraging research on public library issues and problems.
- Publications of *Grandhana*, *RRRLF news letter* and other publications.
- Establishment of four zonal offices in four parts of the country.

## LIBRARY LEGISLATION

The RRRLF since its inception has been persuading and insisting on the state governments to enact public library legislation. Due to its efforts the public library legislation has been enacted in West Bengal (1979), Manipur (1988) Kerala (1989), Haryana (1989), Mizoram (1987), Goa (1994) Gujarat (2003) Assam (2005-2006), Orissa (2005) and Uttar Pradesh (2006), Rajasthan (2009) and Bihar (2008). Still it is continuing its efforts to convince the state governments in the remaining states and union territories to enact the public legislation in the country.

## NATIONAL POLICY FOR PUBLIC LIBRARIES (NAPLIS)

The UNESCO in its publication "*Guidelines on information policy*", insisted its member states to publish their policy for public libraries. The Government of India appointed a committee in 1985 under the Chairmanship of Prof. D.P. Chattapadhaya for drafting a comprehensive NAPLIS. The

Director of the RRRLF was the convenor of the committee and helped it in formulating its recommendations. The draft policy was submitted to the government and the RRRLF has been pursuing the Government of India to adopt this policy on par with the National Educational Policy, the National Science Policy, and the National Industrial Policy etc. The Draft policy is still pending with the Government of India. It had recently appointed a Knowledge Commission to review the entire scenario in the country and submit its recommendations on public libraries. The Commission had submitted its report.

## Survey of The RRRLF on Public Libraries

The RRRLF established four Zonal Offices in the four zones of the country. The Administrative Officers in the Zonal Offices who are professionals in Library and Information Science regularly visit all the public libraries in their zonal jurisdiction and inform their headquarters about the state of affairs on public libraries. Further the RRRLF recently got a survey conducted on the state of conditions of the public libraries by a private organization viz. A.C. Neilson Org. Marg Pvt. Ltd. The report stated that only 49,757 villages have libraries, out of 5,57,137 villages in the country. This reveals that only 9 per cent of villages are having public libraries and per captia income incurred on public libraries is only Rs.0.07ps. The RRRLF based on the AC. Neilson Org. Marg report classified the states into three categories namely 1) Lagging 2) Developing 3) Developed. So the RRRLF from time to time either directly or through agencies has been conducting surveys on the public libraries in the country. *The Neilson Org. Marg Survey Report* pointed out the following perceptions towards the RRRLF initiatives by the libraries

- Majority of the libraries perceived that the RRRLF schemes are instrumental to solve the problems faced by the public libraries.
- Different categories of respondents perceived that the RRRL initiatives are the only effort in it's nature for the

betterment of the public library system in the country.

- Substantial number of respondents perceived that the beneficiary library would run into deep trouble in case the RRRLF stops assistance.
- Majority of public libraries advocate that the RRRLF should increase assistance and take more initiatives
- Substantial number of respondents perceived that the RRRLF needs to communicate their schemes more explicitly to the beneficiaries, so that they can avail them depending upon their need and eligibility.

## RRRLF Initiatives for the Establishment of Public Libraries

The RRRLF- has been pursuing the state governments to give priority and to provide funds for the establishment of public libraries in more and more villages. It provided funds for purchasing land, construction of buildings and also acquisition of required furniture. Through the efforts of the RRRLF several village libraries were established in the villages with its financial assistance to the states. The Foundation has taken long strides in promoting library services in the country. It has been spending more than 35 crores annually for the growth and development of the public libraries in the country.

## Matching Grants to the States

The RRRLF provides matching grants to every state annually for purchase of books, furniture, and computers etc. If a state government gives 50 per cent of the estimated expenditure, the RRRLF provides the remaining 50 per cent of the expenditure. The RRRLF provides assistance for the following programmes of the public libraries.

- Assistance towards organization of seminars, workshops, training courses (orientation/refresher) awareness programmes and book exhibitions.
- Assistance towards supply of storage and display materials and reading room furniture.

- Assistance towards development of Rural Book Deposit Centers and Mobile Library Services.
- Assistance to public libraries for increasing accommodation.
- Assistance to public libraries for acquiring TV-cum-VCP sets for educational purposes/computers for application to libraries.
- Assistance to voluntary organizations providing public library services.
- Assistance to children's libraries and children's sections of general Public libraries.
- Assistance towards organization of seminar/conference by the national level organizations.
- Assistance to libraries towards celebration of Golden Jubilee year/ Platinum Jubilee year/Centenary year/125 year/150 year/175 year and the like.
- Assistance towards collection and compilation of library statistics through official and non-official agencies.
- Assistance towards establishment of the RRRLF children's corner.
- Assistance towards development of District Youth Resource Centers.

**Aid for Construction of Buildings for Public Libraries in the States and Union Territories**

State governments in general lack finances for the development of public library infrastructure. Building for a public library in villages is an important component. Philanthropists have been coming forward to give land for the construction of library buildings in the villages but the Directorate of Public Libraries are not in a position to meet the expenditure for the construction of the library buildings. The RRRLF has come forward to extend financial assistance in such cases. A village library without a building is a difficult proposition. Besides the district sub-divisional and town libraries, the RRRLF has been sanctioning Rs.4 lakh for each rural library. During the period 2007-2008 the Foundation released building grants to 128 public libraries in the country involving an assistance of Rs. 327.09 lakhs. Hence, the RRRLF program to aid the construction of public library buildings is a laudable one.

## Modernization of Public Libraries

The interface of computer technology with the communication technology made the flow of information easier and faster. The networking of public libraries has become essential. In order to bring the latest information to the doorsteps of the clientele, the modernization of public libraries has become inevitable. The RRRLF realized the lack of automation in public libraries. In order to fill in the gap, the RRRLF came forward to provide computers to all State Central Libraries (SCLs) and District Central Libraries (DCLs). It wants to network the SCLs and DCLs in the first phase. It also proposes ultimately to cover and link up all the public libraries, mandal libraries, village libraries and book deposit centres with the DCLs and SCLs. It aims to establish a network of Indian public libraries on the model of JANNET in England so as to satisfy the ever increasing thirst for knowledge and easy access to information by the clientele in the rural communities. The modernization of the public libraries in the villages will enable rural communities to have access to information. It is desirable to establish a photo digital library to help the public libraries.

## Opening New Sections or Reading Corners in Public Libraries

The RRRLF after making various surveys realized that certain sections of rural communities like women and children have not been provided sufficient opportunities for their reading needs in public libraries. Women are important in family development. The neglect of these two sections in the rural communities would weaken the democratic foundation of the

Indian society. The RRRLF has been insisting and also financing the public libraries to open separate sections for woman and children in public libraries. These sections are to be provided with required collection of books and information material. This would result generally in improving the reading habits of rural children and women. The RRRLF during the financial year 2007-2008 released Rs. 32 lakhs for establishing the children and women sections in the public libraries.

### Annual lecture program

The RRRLF arranges annual lectures in various parts of the country in order to create the public library culture and awareness which is lacking at present. These lectures impress on the people on the importance of public libraries among the educated for life long education.

### Assisting LIS Associations and NGOs

The RRRLF assists all library associations at national and state levels to hold conferences, seminars, debates, and workshops on library issues. Such debates and discussions, among various other things, create awareness of the importance of public libraries, village libraries and community information centres in the society.

### Instituting Awards for the Best Public Libraries, Best Librarians and Fellowships

The RRRLF has been giving awards annually to the best public libraries and the best public librarians to motivate the library professionals to render positive services to the people. This provides a sense of enthusiasm in the library staff to provide more and more services to the rural people.

### Training and Refresher Courses to the Library Personnel

Grants are provided by the RRRLF to the Directorates of public libraries in the states to conduct refresher training courses to update the skills of the professionals in the modern technology.

## Encouraging Research Programs on Problems and Issues of Public Libraries

The ultimate goal of the governments in the democratic countries is to establish an information society or a knowledge society. As stated by J.S. Mill that the worth of the State, in the long run, is the worth of the individuals composing it. The RRRLF strives through its different programmes to improve the knowledge of people and the social fabric. It provides funds for conducting research on public libraries. The young and experienced professionals are provided with grants to carry out or to conduct research on public library issues. The feedback enables the RRRLF to reorient its programmes and plans.

## CONCLUSION

The RRRLF is the only national agency undertaking pogrammes and activities for the growth and development of public libraries in India. It is anxious to establish public library network for enriching knowledge base in rural community. The RRRLF hopes to establish libraries in backward areas, tribal areas and forest and hilly areas in order to bring the illiterates, and innocent people into the main stream of public life. The RRRLF has many splendid programs and plans. But its financial budget is scarce and limited. The Government of India should provide the RRRLF at least with 5 to 10 per cent of its annual budget for the development of public libraries in the country. Public libraries should be considered as important as the educational institutions, like schools, colleges and universities. Public libraries are the gateways to information. According to the UNESCO Public Library Manifesto the establishment of public libraries, community information centres is mandatory on the part of the government. Given the poor state of public libraries in the states, the RRRLF should impress on the Central government to bring out a National Public Library Policy document at the earliest. The national policy alone can provide the direction and guidance for the overall development of the public libraries in the country. The establishment of public library network is already delayed in India. The county has already come to witness the emergence of Banks Network, Railway Network, and the INFLIBNET for the academic libraries, but there is no such network for the public libraries in the country. The programs of the RRRLF should be reoriented so that public libraries come to reach the people at the grass root level and more explicitly.

## REFERENCES

1. A C Nielsen Org-Marg Pvt Ltd (2004). Evaluation study of status of public library with reference to the services of RRRLF, Final report, Kolkota (mimeo).
2. Damle, Y.B. (1955). Communication of Modern Ideas and Knowledge: In Indian Villages, Poona: Deccan College.
3. India: Human Resource Development, Ministry of (1986) National Policy on library and information system; A presentation (Chairman: D.P. Chattopadhyay) New Delhi; Committee on National Policy and Information system (Mimeo).
4. India : Human Resources Development, Ministry of—(1990) Towards an enlightened and humane society Report of the committee for review of National Policy on education (NPE) 1986 (Chairman Ramamurti) New Delhi, The Committee.
5. India : Planning Commission, New Delhi (1984). Report of the working group of the planning commission on modernization of library services and informatics for the Seventh Five Year Plan 1988-1990, New Delhi, Planning Commission.
6. Kaul, H.K. (2004). Role of public libraries as knowledge centers in modern society (paper presented at the Raja Ramamohun Roy Library Foundation National Seminar, 14th February 2004) (mimeo).
7. McArthur, Tom (1986), Worlds of reference: Lexico graphs, learning and language from the clay tablet to the computer, Cambridge: CUP.

8. Mahapatra, P.K. and Thomas, V.K. eds (1996). Public libraries in developing countries; status and trends (Dr B.P. Barua Festschrift Volume) New Delhi; Vikas publishing House.
9. Raja Rammohun Roy Library Foundation, Kolkota (2008). Agenda; 73rd meeting of the Foundation, January 21,2008 Kolkata: The Foundation (1993)
10. ______. Books for the Millions at their Doorsteps "Information Manual" 5th Edition, 1997.
11. ______. Memorandum of Association and Rules" 2nd ed, 1972.
12. ______. Two Decades of the Foundation, 1972-1992, Kolkata; The Foundation.

# 6

# The Dying Culture of Reading Habit in Public Libraries in India in the Digital Age : The Socio-economic and Technological Factors

*"If language is not correct then what is said is not what is meant, if what is said is not what is meant then what ought to be done remains undone"* — **Confucius**

Man has acquired certain embodiments which are unique in nature. Language, Script and Reading are special gifts. Since the days of acquisition of language and script man began to communicate in writing. He started using different media such as clay tablets, stone, bones, papyrus, parchment, velum, cloth, birch barks, palm leaf, copper plates and hand made paper. The production of such documents was not only time-consuming but also very expensive. Libraries consisting of such documents could therefore be established only by ruling kings and by wealthy religious institutions.

A paradigm shift has taken place in human history in 1454 when Johann Gutenberg discovered the movable type. Both Gutenberg and Caxton spanned the entire Europe with printing of books . The printing of the *Penny Bible* and other religious books took Europe into the present phase of modern civilization. Books replaced the oral communication and other types of communication. Books brought many advantages. Some of them are:

- People began to acquire books for their personal reding
- Education began to spread.
- Communication became easier
- Copying of books by scholars and monks discountinued
- Diaspora of ideas and concepts began to flow from one continent to the other cutting across time and space
- Science and technology began to emerge replacing the religious dogma and fundamentalism
- Literacy has increased and the reding habit among the literate has become common
- Books generated more books with clash of ideas, cultures and classes
- Book became powerful than sword and it led to democratic ideas
- Rosseau's ideas, Marx's *The capital* and Bankimchand's *Anandmath* (Vandemataram) had led to the French Revolution, the Russian Revolution and the Indian Movement for independence respectively.
- Books were instrumental for Book Fairs such as Lyons Book Fairs, Frankfurt Book Fairs etc, which brought books nearer to people
- Circulation libraries, Junto libraries subsequently led the

establishement of public libraries in the 19$^{th}$ century through out the civilized world.

The printing revolution led to the increased reading habit. The reading habit provides access to information which enriches people with knowledge and wisdom. The impact of reading on people is complex. Francis Bacon, therefore, rightly said that, "reading maketh a full man" Abraham Lincoln once said that, "the things I want to know , are in books . My friend is a man who will get a book I ain't read", So at the beginning of the modern civilization i.e. 16$^{th}$ to 19$^{th}$ centuries, reading books had been a craze, habit, mania, hobby, necessity and an essential activity. The powerful compulsions in the general public led to the establishment of public libraries. The first public library legislation was passed by the British paliament in August 1850. Even the UNESCO Manifesto says that the establishment of the Public Libraries is mandatory on the part of governments, so they came to be established in every country, more so in all democratic countries. Central or State Governments and also both together have been spending huge amounts for the establishment of more and more public libraries. Inspite of their best efforts there are more habitations in India which don't have public libraries. The complete coverage of villages with the public libraries today looks like the Will-o-the-wisp or a mirage.

The question here is not the reading habit, which is increasing with literacy. It should bloom a thousand fold more. The question that is confronting us is how many people are utilizing this public library facility. In 1950 Helen Haines wrote in *Living with Books* stated that there is astonishing reading crises in America in the worlds most financially and politically developed nation. Is there not decline in the real and serious resders visiting the public libraries in our country? If So, why is it so? Then what are the measures to be taken to make the public libraries modern, more attractive and useful to all sections of people in the society. The causes of the malaise and the factors of alienation of the people from the public libraries should be thoroughly analyzed and examined. The disease is deeper. There are many factors. However, it is only economic, sociological and technological factors are examined below threadbare:

## ECONOMIC FACTORS

### Povery

There is stark poverty in certain parts of the country and certain sections of society. Their entire day to day effort is to work for food and to live. Nearly 50% of Indian population is at or below poverty line.

### Information As A Resource

People in general in India consider the land and capital as important resources. Information is not still considered as an jmportant resource. Information only converts other resources into power and profit.

### Finances

The finances available for the development of the public library system is negligible. There is no direct budgetary provision for libraries in the State or Central annual budgets. Governments are spending huge capital resources for various purposes but not for library digital connectivity. Take the case of Andhra pradesh, there are 29 thousand inhabitations , whereas there are only 3,500 government libraries. It means that there are nearly 25 thousand inhabitations without public libraries, which are information outlets for the people. The conditions in other states also is no better. The governments are indifferent to provide finances to the pulic libratries.

### Prices of Books And Periodicals

Prices of books and periodicals were low earlier. Academic Insititutions, bodies, organizations and academics use to publish books on no-profit and no-loss basis in order the books and periodicals are available to people at large. This concept is given a go-bye. Prices of books and periodicals have increased hundred fold. Most of the Public libraries are not able to purchase all important books and periodicals useful to their readers.

### Travel

In cities and towns to reach the town libraries or State Central Library involves considerable expenditure. Poor and middle class people cannot afford it. The branch libraries and book centres are chaotic and don't have satisfactory collections. Research scholars find it expensive to go to the National Libraries and other important libraries in distant cities like kolkata, Delhi, Chennai and Mumbai.

### Library Buildings And Infrastructure

Construction and expansion of library buildings is a recurring expenditure constantly incurred. These eat away most of the finances of the libraries. The expenditure on buildings and salaries for manpower has become a heavy one and the goverments shy away to open new village libraries.

## SOCIOLOGICAL FACTORS

As foretold in Alvin Toffler's books, *Future Shock, Third wave* and *Power Shift*, swift and silent changes have taken place in social systems. People's mind sets have been undergoing changes. Their psychology and attitudes towards reading habit and efforts to access to knowledge have undergone radical transformation.

- People do not have patience to read big tomes. These days we hardly come caross any youth who are interested to read books like *Veyipadagalu* (Sahasrapani), *Ulysses* and *Decline and Fall of the Roman Empire.* People are intrested in short discourses, stories etc.
- Readership to creative writing like poetry, drama and novel is on decline. Even housewives who were used to

read novels and stories during their leisure time have slowly given up their hobby reading and have shifted to Television seeing.

- Students and children have diverted their attention to computer games.
- Mass media like Radio, T.V, Video, Films and Computer have their impact on the reading habits of people. People in the earlier days, used to read at home during their leisure hours, but now their attention is more drawn towards Television and Computer channels to see serials, news, films and other entertianment programmes. Television programmes and computer surfing hardly allow time to people to read serious stuff.
- Due to severe competition for professional courses like Medicine, Engineering etc. students spend most of their time to read text books and to attend special coaching classes. They hardly find any time to read general books, literary and religious classics. They hardly find time to go to the public libraries for general reading.
- In the past to go to libraries and to read books was a symbol of intellectualism. Book in-hand was a status symbol. These days middle class and rich class people abhor to go to the libraries. It is below their dignity. Only lower middle class and poor people visit libraries to read newspapers, magazines and text books etc. because they cannot afford to purchase them.
- To earn more money is today's motto than to learn more, even though we talk of the Information Society and Knowledge Society.
- ILLETERACY: 40 per cent of our population are illiterates. Out of the other 60 per cent also, most of the people are smatterers. They only know to write and read their names. This illiteracy problem is stalking our country and holding up its progress. They don't naturally find libraries useful.

## TECHNOLOGICAL FACTORS

In the second half of the $20^{th}$ century, there are revolutionary changes in Communication and Information Technology (CIT). Computer and Internet made the world a Global Village.

- E-Books and E-Journals have brought changes in library collections. Big series like *The Encyclopaedia Britannica* and the *Oxford English Dictionary* are available in CD disk. Their price is low and even individuals can buy them. People have become computer humans.
- Huge collections can be compressed into few DVD's, which can be carried away from any where to any where in a brief case.
- Web sites and Networking of libraries made people to download materials sitting at home without going to any library.
- Networks like UNITY, RLIN, UCLC, INFLIBNET, DELNET, CALIBNET etc. facilitate to bring any documents to peoples working desks without any botheration of visiting umpteen libraries in the country and abord.
- Collection of data on any subject is easier through the Net than visiting to libraries and collecting it physically.

All serious scholars, scientists, managers, business executives for all and sundry information, approach their P.Os than asking their librarians and Information Scientists. In course of another century, there may be the paperless society visualized by Lancaster. Future children may start using their computers for learning and information than the public libraries. Public libraries may stand in isolation as models of beauty of the pre internet era. Public libraries have to change drastically otherwise they will die like many medieval institutions. It is the responsibility of the Librarians and Information Scientists to stop the present rot and decline of the public libraries.

## REFERENCES

1. BRONOWESKI, Jacob. The ascent of man. London; BBC, 1973.
2. CASTELLS, Manuel. The Information city: Information Technology, Economic Restructuring and the Urban-Regional process. London; Basil Blackwell, 1989.
3. CAWKELL, A.E (ed.) Evolution of Information Society. London: ASLIB, 1987.
4. FOSKETT, D.J.(ed.) The Information Environment: A World view. London;Elsever, 1990.
5. GUILIANO, V.F. (et et). Into the Information Age: A perspective for federal action. Chicago:ALA, 1978.
6. IFLA. The Impact of Information Technology upon Public Libraries. The Hague: IFLA. 1985. Public Library guidelines. The Hague: IFLA, 2000.
7. LANCASTER, F.W. Future Librarianship: Preparing for an Unconventional carrer. *Wilson Library Bulletin,* 1993. pages 747-753. Towards paperless Information systems. Newyork: Academic press, 1978.
8. Mac BRIDE, Sean (et al) Many voces, One world: Towards a New More Just More efficient-world Information and Communication order. London: KoganPage, 1980.
9. McARTHUR, Tom. Worlds of Reference. Cambridge: CUP, 1986.
10. MAZLISH, Bruce The Fourth discontinuty The Co-evolution of Humans and the Machines. New Havens: Yale University press, 1993.
11. MCGARY, K.J. The Changing context of Information. London: Clive Bingley. 1981.
12. RAMAIAH, L.S. To Make reading a habbit, Way of life. *The Hindu* 16-10-1990. page 19.
13. Use of tools and machines in libraries in the past, present and in the future: A retrospect and a Fancy. *In* To Greater heights. New Delhi: ESS ESS publications, 2003. pages 151-153.
14. THOMAS, V.K. Computerization of public libraries in India. *Grandhana* 9:1-2 (2002) pp 55-64.

15. VENKATAPPAIAH, Velaga. Digital Public Libraries: The need for Today and Tomorrow. *Granthana* 9:1-2(2002) PP 47-54.
16. WEISMAN, Herman M. Information Systems, Services and Centres. Newyork: Becker and Hayes, 1972.

# 7

# Records and Archieves : What are They?

## INTRODUCTION

The progress of man from the primitive times to the present day is a great *saga*. During this period of evolution he accquired certain skills which had changed the course of human life greatly. They are 1. Speech; 2. Script, 3. Printing and 4. Automation. The entire human epistemology or gnosiology is derived from them. Man used variety of material from clay tablets to computers to write or record his thoughts. These materials which are housed in Museums, Record Offices or Archives and Libraries, are man's memory banks. They are our cultural assets too.

Records constitute one of the world's primary information sources. Often the terms Records and Archieves are used as synonyms. Records is a generic term. All archieves are records but all records are not archives. Let us, therefore, see what are records and what are archives, and what distingusihes them one from another.

## RECORDS

The word record comes from the Latin word ***recordari***

meaning to be mindful of. This again originates from the Latin word **cor** which means heart. The only relationship between 'heart' and being mindful of being that at one time the heart was believed to be the seat of man's memory. We have, hence, the expression 'to learn by heart'.

The OED gives a number of definitions of the word[1] records' all of which emphasize that a record is something committed to writting in order to preserve the memory of a fact or a event. The record presupposes a record creator who can be an individual, a family, an institution, a commercial or other organisation or a government agency. The specific purpose can be in pursuance of a legal requirement or in connection with the transaction of creator's business. Records, therefore, are the books, papers, maps, photographs or other documentary materials regardless of physical form or characteristics made or received by a government agency, institution or organisation, family or individual in pursuance of law or in connection with the transaction of their business and preserved by them or their successors. In modern times, government at all levels is by far the greatest record creator. Fig. 1 shows the forms of records.

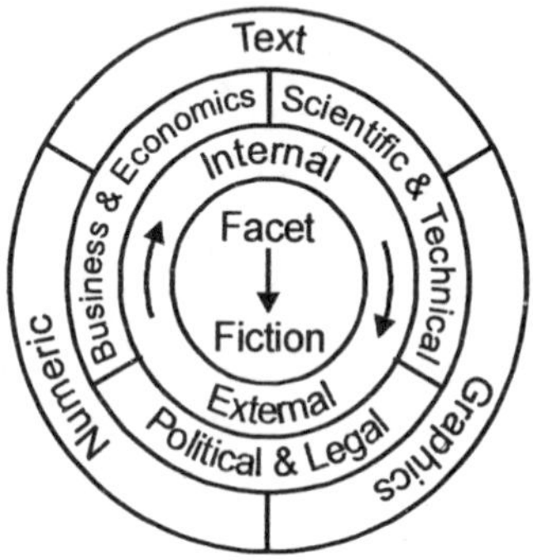


**Fig. 1**

Organisations, individuals and governments use both internal and external information in decision making. Some analysis, experience and judgement were mixed with the available information for this purpose. (See Fig. 2).

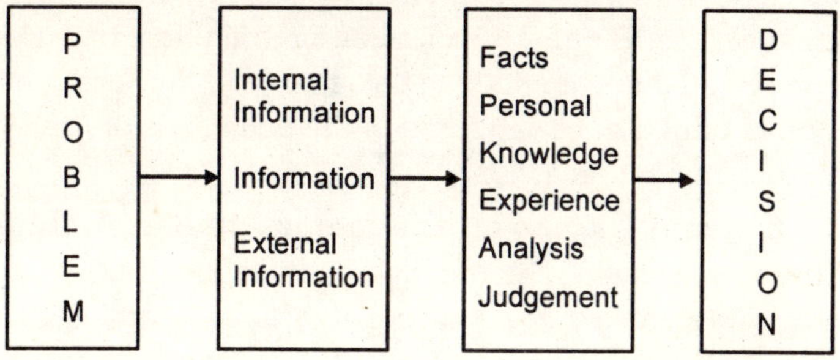


**Fig. 2**

## ARCHIVES

The second term 'Archives' has derived from the Greek word '*archeion*' meaning that which belongs to an office. *Archeion* has its origin in the word *arche* which has a number of meanings, and consequently a number of derivatives with different connotations. *Arche* means (1) beginning, origin, first cause; (2) first place, power, sovereignty, empire, realm; and (3) magistrates office. From the first of these sets derived the Greek *archaios* meaning old, ancient, etc. and from this we have such derivatives as archaic, archeology. From the second set is derived *architekton* from which we get architect, archibishop. From the third set is derived the word *archaion*. From this Greek word, the Latin word *archivum* was derived. From the Latin word *archivum,* the French words *archive* and *les archives* have come. From these French words the English word archives has come. In the English language, the term archives has atleast three distinct things : (1) the records themselves; (2)the building which houses the records; and (3)the administrative set-up responsible for the maintenance of the records. Let us restrict the meaning of the word to records leavings out the other two meanings, viz., the building and the administrative set-up.

Historical manuscripts, isolated letters of ancient rulers, copper plates, stone inscriptions besides a host of other things are popularly known as archives, Strictly speaking archives do not include them in their field. Archives are a greater or a lesser fraction of records of an organisation or institution, etc. which are preserved for their enduring value whether they are current or non-current. Let us see some of the definitions of Archives given by eminent archivists.

**Eugenio Casanova, the famous Italian Archivist defines archives** : "The orderly accumulation of documents which were created in the course of its activity by an institution or an individual and which are preserved for the accomplishment of its political, legal or cultural purposes by such an institution or individual."

**Adolf Brenneke, the German Archivist, has defined archives** : "The whole of the papers and documents growing out of legal or buisness activities of a physical or legal body which are intended for permanent preservation at a particular place as the source and evidence of the past."

Dr. P. Basu, an eminent Indian Archivist, says that "Archives are records of enduring value no longer required by the creating agency for frequent reference."

It is thus clear that the archives are essentially all records but all records are not archives.

## SPECIAL CHARACTERISTICS OF ARCHIVES

There are four characteristics which distinguish archives from the other reference materials. The first characteristic is the relationship that archives bear to the creating agency. The archives of a particular agency or institution are intended to reflect the policies, functions and transactions of that agency alone and nothing else. From this fact that the first principle of the archive administration is derived. It is that *the archives of a given creator should in no circumstances be intermingled with those of another creator.*

The second characterisitc is the official character of archives being products or by-products of transactions having legal effects. From this the second priciple of the archive administration was derived. It is that *the archives must remain in the unbroken custody of the creator or his legitmate successor for their validity in the court of law.*

The third characteristic of the archives is their uniqueness. Each record is created in single copy for one specific purpose.

The fourth characteristic is the organicity of the archives. This refers to the underlying fact that they are not collected, in the usual sense of the term, by the originating organisation or agency but rather grow naturally out of their activities and operations. Each piece in a file is organically connected with the preceding and succeding pieces in the file. If they are torn from each other, they may not give wholly accurate information and probably may give wholly inaccurate information. Thus, the individual units that make-up an organizational archives do not exist independandtly but instead are integrated within an overall structure of documentation that is essential to their significance.Hence, the archives administration stipulates the sanctity of the original order, This leads logically to the fundamental *principle of provenance* or *respect des fonds*.

The library materials and other referenece materials don't have the above characteristics. Books in a general library or items in a historical manuscript library are collections of isolated pieces. They are arranged in some logical order after their collection. Archives, on the other hand, are accumulations. Their order and arrangement are determined as they grow. Other materials don't possess official character which is essential in the case of archives.

## CLASSES OF RECORDS AND ARCHIVES

Records and archives can be classified under the following categories :

1. According to the creator.
2. According to the form.

3. According to the logitimate use
4. According to the state of compilation
5. According to the subject matter.
6. According to the importance.
7. According to the chronological limits.

- From the point of the creating agency, archives can be classified into three categories, viz., public, semi-public and private.
- From the point of view of their form archives can be classified as textual, cartographic and numeric.
- The next type of classification is in accordance with their legitmate use, that open records and closed records. All such records which have been thrown open for bonafide research and for inspection by the public come under the category of open records. All such archives to which public and research scholars are not allowed access come under the category of closed records.
- Another important basis of classification of archives is according to the state of their compilation, i.e., current, semi-current and non-current.
- The classification of archives in accordance with the subject matter implies the grouping of records dealing with particular subjects. Thus we may have revenue records, judicial records, so on and so forth. This type of library classification owed its origin to the influence of library science and was in vogue with respect to the archives in France before the formation of archival principles of provenance.
- The classification of archives according to their importance implies their division into three categories, namely *A*, *B* and *C*. The papers which, deal with policy matters, important decisions and organisational history and administrative landmarks are categorised as *A* class

papers. Those dealing with operational part are placed under *B* category. Papers of routine nature are classed as *C* class papers. Before the introduction of the modern filing system, we had this classification of records. The greatest advantage of this classification is that the task of appraisal and ultimate weeding of records is made easy.

- The classification of archives in accordance with chronological limits is most advantageous for such collections as are very big and cover a long period,The above are some of the principles on which records and archives can be classified, depending upon their bulk, nature and contents.

## FINDING AIDS

Records and archives are preserved for their enduring values. The main business of various institutions, therefore, is the proper arrangement of records and archives and their availability. In order to locate the required records and archives and to retrieve the information needed by users, search tools or Finding Aids are essential for every archives or record office. The Finding Aids prepared in archives/records office for internal use and for the use of researchers are : (1) Inventory; (2) The File List; (3) Transfer List; (4) Check List ; (5) Guides ; (6) Handbook ; (7) Desciptive List ; (8) Indexing ; and (9) Calendaring.

**Inventory :** The Inventory is nothing but the written or printed description of archives under suitable organisational heads and sub-heads. It is an initial finding aid. The inventory is a stock register of records. An inventory should normally cover all records that come within a particular record group. Two types of inventories are generally prepared for public records, (a) one in which the record series are merely indentified by tittles; and (b) the other in which records series are identified and described.

**The File List :** This list is required for internal use just to indicate the physical existance of the file in a particular collection. The subject of the file is rarely indicated in this list.

**Transfer List :** A Transfer List is prepared at the time of actual transfer of records from the creating agency to the Archives/records office.

**Check List** : After the preparation of the Transfer List the records are transferred to the archives/records office for custody and on the basis of this transfer list the files are checked. As a result of such checking a check list is prepared.

**Guide** : A guide is a description of a collection or a group of records, the purpose of which is to indicate to the user of records the general contents of the collection specifying their arrangement and the nature of subject that they deal with.

**Handbook** : Handbook is a detailed guide to archives enumerating the departments, branches and giving detailed information about their records.

**Descriptive List** : Scholars would like to have a precise idea as to the contents of every document relating to the period of his research. The descriptive list lays emphasis on the subject of the document which is brought out in the form of summary. A descriptive list contains three parts, viz., 1. Preface; 2. Text; and 3. Index. The descriptive lists are generally prepared for important collections or series.

**Indexing** : In archival repositories information is located and retrieved with the help of a good index. There are two types of indexes. One is prepared by the Department in which the records originated. In this index the subject headings are arranged alphabetically in accordance with a catch word. They are prepared separetely by each of the sections, branches in a Department/Ministry indicating matters of administrative importance.

When the records are centralised in an archives or records office, the need for preparation of a detailed indexes is often felt. In such indexes due notice is taken of place names, personal names and the subject of each document. It makes a specialised study of each document to bring out all its details. Though the preparation of these indexes is laborious, expensive and time-consuming, they are comprehensive and valuable for the use of research scholars. There are certain rules for preparing an index :

- The indexer should have complete knowledge of the subject matter of the document.
- The document should be personally examined.
- Then the indexer should decide upon the details he wants to incorporate in his index slips.
- The indexer should prefer the short word to the long word, the direct word to the indirect word, the concrete word to the abstract word and the familiar word to the unfamiliar word.
- Spelling is to be modernised. Standard tools should be used for the place names and personal names.
- The headings in an index are to be arranged alphabetically and entries under them chronologically.
- The references to be cited after the entries are to the department, the date, the month, the year and the number of the document.
- The index should be provided with a glossary to explain obsolete and unfamiliar words.

**Calendaring** : Calendaring is a process of shortening a document by means of omission of non-essential parts. This is a sort of editing, This is an expanded form of the descriptive listing.

In developed countries the archival/record institutions developed their plans and computer programmes for indexing from the experience of libraries. The Library of Congress, while developing the National Union Catalogue of Manuscript

Collections constructed a thesaurus for manuscript indexing. Then the Herbert-Hoover Archives also compiled a controlled vocablury for indexing. The Manuscript Division of the Library of Congress employed SPINDEX (Selective Permutation Index) for retrieval of manuscript by names, subjects, collection name and container location. The SPINDEX was an adaptation from the IBM KWIC (Key word in context) software.

## ACCESSIBILITY TO RECORDS/ARCHIVES AND THEIR USE FOR ADMINISTRATION AND RESEARCH

Public access to the archives/records is relatively a modern concept. It is linked up with the progress of both deomocracy and objective historical research. For the first time the archives were opened to public in 1794 after the French Revolution. The policies of access to public records vary from nation to nation, and sometimes within a nation too. The International Council on Archives at its Congresses held in 1966 and 1968 had strongly urged for the liberalization of access policies. Most of the countries allow access to their records which are more than 30 to 50 years old, with special provision to ensure the protection of individual privacy and state security.

The fundamental purpose of the archival or records work is to preserve permanently valuable records and make them available for use. The activities involved in providing access to records constitute the archival institution's reference service. It consists of furnishing records for use in search rooms, providing information from records and concerning records, making copies of records, lending records to certainArchives/ records are preserved and maintained by the creating agency, either government departments or private institutions, for their own administrative reference puposes. These bodies keep them as evidence of their origin, organization, policies, programmes and principal operations over time. They are also kept for legel and financial purposes. Governments and administrators use archives/records as precedents in taking policy decisions and to justify their actions. The archives/records are useful to the administrators to justify themselves if need arises before law courts.

There are others who use the archives/records besides the creating agencies. Private individuals and unofficial bodies use them to safeguard rights of various kinds. Records of municipalities and local bodies are evidence of the rights of citizens or of their obligations to fellow citizens. Birth, marriage and death records have bearing on the question of citizenship. Records relating to transfer of property are needed to clear-up disputed inheritence cases. Electoral rolls give evidence to the right of people to participate in the government of the country. Finally, the citizen can, from the records, check-up on how his representative has shared in running the government and how his hard earned money paid in the shape of taxes has been spent.

Because of the density of information available in records and archives, they are huntings grounds for researchers in the social sciences primarily, but also in the physical sciences in pursing their researches.

## REFERENCES

1. Burner Richard C : 1983. Archival Theory and Practices in the United States: A Historical Analysis, Seattle, University of Washington Press.
2. Carbone Salvator and Raoul Gueze : 1972. Draft Model Law on Archives : Description and Text. Paris, Unesco.
3. Jankinson Sir Hilary : 1965. A Manual of Archive Administration. 2nd ed.
4. Shellenberg T.R. : The Management of Archives.
5. Schellengberg T.R.: 1956. Modem Archives: Principles and Techniques.

# 8

# Computerization of Archival Holdings of Open Period in India

## INTRODUCTION

The present day world, without doubt has changed very rapidly in the recent years. At the same time the life style of the people too has changed tremendously. Many symbols of modern civilization, a few decades ago, like Radio, Telephone, Bicycle, Calculator, Type Writer, Tape-recorder, Gramphone etc., have been replaced by the people to Televisions, Stereo Decks, Cellular Phones, VCR and VCD and finally Computers. Due to development of new technologies, the computers now available in the market pertains to fifth generation useful to the people in numerous ways in discharge of their functions in a speedy manner.

The improvement brought in the computers like high capacity hard disks for storage of more information on computer memory, chip system made the work easier in the companies, banks, administration and industries all over the world. In addition to the super computers, and laptop computers, palm top computers are available to the business men, bureaucrats, and even ordinary people A new work culture has developed, as more and more people including school children are dependent on computers. In the age of information technology, the computer is a gifted machine for the service of mankind.

Under the process of modernization, many nations have adopted computer education in schools, colleges and universities, computer net-working and soft-ware packages in their organizations whether it is government or private for proper functioning of these bodies. The computerization process is still continuing as information technology developed vastly covering all the subjects, and people wanted to use computer applications where ever the same has not been applied so far. In India, computer networking and software packages have been introduced in a limited way in the Ministries, Government Departments, Banks and Industries. However, computerization is already invogue in the railways, post offices, Air and bus travel, schools, colleges and universities, business houses and even private organizations.

The computer thus, has come to be a part and parcel in the lives of the people. The computer net-working and the software packages, helps an organization in several ways particularly administering in a better way in maintaining service records, conducting useful conferences, accounts, records of stores purchased and discharge of functions relating to the organization in an efficient manner.

Any information needed by the administrators whether it is scientific or technological or information about the service records, or on any other subject could be retrieved without loss of time. This facility of making available any information to the top brass including precedents of any case would help them to arrive at a quick decision and speedy disposal of the cases. As speed in the work of organizations has acquired prominence, the use of computers is a must without any semblance of doubt.

## ARCHIVES

In any country, Public Libraries and Archival Institutions are very important for social, academic and economic development. The library is a well known place in any village, town and city. Archives as defined by the Oxford English Dictionary are 'a place in which public records kept'. According to an eminent Indian Archivist Dr. Purnendu Basu 'Archives are records of enduring values, no longer required by the creating agency for frequent use'. In India, the rulers of the country both in ancient and medieval periods used to record important events of their regime or grants to temples or individuals as stone inscriptions and copper plates. But these are stray documents of historical value and do not constitute archives.

Eugino Casanova, an Italian Archivist stated that 'archives are orderly accumulations of documents which were created in the course of its activity by an institution or individual and which are preserved for the accomplishment of its political or legal and cultural purposes by such an individual or institution'. Hence, it may be stated that the archives are permanent records transferred to an archival department by the creating agency and the holdings are preserved in that institution in perpetuity for various uses.

Archives of an agency or department or Ministry reflect the policies, functions and the transactions of that organization. The archival documents are unique and precious and once lost cannot be replaced, as each document or file is created as a single copy and that too for a specified purpose.

Archives are not being collected by the creating agency, but grow naturally due to the activities of the organizations or governments, industries, business houses or academic institutions. The archives contain information on various subjects and are primary sources for information needed for reference purposes to the administrator's, legal and judicial purposes and also to the scholarly world for conducting research on various topics. Archives are classified according to the sources of their origin generally known as the principle of provenance.

**Organization of Archives**

In our country, the National Archives of India, New Delhi is the custodian of all Government of India records of permanent value. The department was established in March 1891 and the institution preserves millions of files of different departments of the government, microfilms and private archival collections. Some of these documents are more than three hundred years old. The State Governments have established their own archives departments and the departments are located in the respective state capitals. According to the Secretariat Manual of the Official Procedure, all non-current files retained by the government as permanent records after twenty five years are required to be transferred to the National Archives of India.

These are *A* and *B* category files recorded as such by the record creating departments or Ministries, and the files survived the review undertaken after the 25th year of their life are to be transferred to the National Archives. Similar system exists for transfer of records periodically from the Secretariat Departments to the State Archives and the files are usually recorded as G.O. Miscellaneous and R.Dis categories in case of files of Heads of Departments under Tottenham System of records management. In 1993, the Indian Parliament passed "The Public Records Act" and later rules were framed and circulated making the transfer of all permanent records of Government of India and its Undertakings to National Archives of India obligatory-The State Governments also may bring similar legislation in the coming years.

The transfer of more records to the archives departments year after year necessitates the construction of new buildings for storage of archival holdings on the lines of developed nations like the U.S.A., U.K. France, Germany and Australia. New technologies are required to be introduced for preservation of records under utmost scientific conditions and also for referencing system. Now a days there is need to preserve electronic records also like Tele-text, E-mail, Voice mail, Fax sheets, Multimedia, CD-Roms, Optical Disks etc., by the Archives Departments, as the proper preservation and up-to-date referencing system are more important works to be undertaken by the organizations on priority basis.

For a referencing system with an object of quick retrieval of files or documents, computers with large sized hard disks are necessary for digitization of reference media or archival holdings. The work relating to digitalization of library books has commenced in most of the libraries of India. The record creating agencies or departments prepare indexes to their records at the closing of their files. However, the Archives departments are preparing reference media to the records in some cases after transfer of records to these institutions.

The archival institutions of India both at Central Government and States have initiated programmes for computerization of the reference media to the holdings. Earlier, reference media such as Indexes, Descriptive lists, Guides to Records have been brought out in the National Archives of India and other State Archives for the benefit of administrators as well as scholars for reference purpose. While doing the work of computerization of reference media, the firms entrusted with this work also scan the title pages of files or proceeding volumes of minutes etc. In this way, physical verification of all the files and documents transferred to the Archives department are analyzed and fed into computer memory. Simultaneously, the computerization of library books in the reference libraries of Archival Institutions has also been undertaken in most of the cases.

Still much work is yet to be done in the Archival Institutions of India with regard to computerization of archival holdings, and we may follow the example of the United States of America, United Kingdom, France and other European countries and New Zealand, Australia and even Malaysia. However, very little information is available about the Archives of China, Korea, Japan, Thailand and Indonesia.

In the countries where web sites exist for the archives of open period [to the files and archival documents] and are thrown open to the scholars for research purposes without restrictions, several facilities are available. Once computerization of archival holdings in the institution has taken place, the information on all subjects including the proper names and place names as mentioned in the indexes is available with comprehensive notes or write -ups to the scholars.

On requisition, the Archives department is in a position to supply the print out of the information sought for as early as possible, no doubt after collecting the usual fee. At the same time, the files indented by the scholars who are conducting research personally in an archival institution, are supplied immediately, as the exact location *of* the series of files including the rack numbers, shelf numbers, and other relevant information are already available on computer memory.

## DEVELOPMENTS IN THE UNITED STATES OF AMERICA

In the publication, *Public Records On Line,* brought out in the United States of America, several advantages on computerization of archival holdings have been enumerated. According to the author, in case of computerization it is possible to find a missing person, locate an asset of the individual's finance position, check the background of an individual or business, compile market lists of the product etc., There are thousands of public record and public information sources accessible to any one in the U.S.A. with a computer and networking. Public Records searching on line is one of the fastest growing areas within the information industry in that country. According to the latest interpretation, public records are the records of incidents.

The incident could be the action by a court, a submission of an application for a specific purpose, or registration of a marriage. The present day society is dependent on information particularly in business and personal inter-action. More advantages have been analyzed like that in the government as well as in the private industry the record-keeping is absolutely necessary to regulate, license and hire the services.

The individual and entities create a trial of information in the daily life starting from the issue of birth certificate of the citizens. The records will help the citizens in many other ways. In short, the public records online is intended to probe the public records, analyze the records type and categorize their application and uses and tell the needy scholars and the public in general regarding the search of records more effectively.

In the United States of America, many government departments and software companies [private] have put the information available in indexes to public records and into data bases. In this venture, the private companies are more enterprising in making the information available to every citizen of the country. The indexes were purchased by them from the government departments and later the companies added more information in such a way the same is useful to the public.

After processing the data, the software companies made information available for a price on individual personal computers either through online connection or on C.D.ROM. This kind of information mostly relate to government agencies, and state motor vehicle department.

In addition, many government departments sell data such as workers compensation, and vehicle records in bulk to private companies. These companies are distributing the information online or on C.D.ROM for a fee.

Further, there are local document retrieval companies in

each state and they obtain the needed information for individual citizen. Generally/ information relating to the borrowing money, setting up of a company or corporation, voter's registration, purchase of a house or a vehicle, involvement of individuals in court cases, and obtaining a drivers license etc., is most useful to the common citizen. Some of the private [software] companies make public record information available (via) internet on a per transaction fee basis.

## INFORMATION VENDORS AND WEB-SITES

The development of World Wide Web [www] is an important stage in the development of Information Technology. The webs can be accessioned though Search Engines like Lycos, Yahoo, etc., through the Internet. The web pages are to be prepared by the parent Archival Organization or Institution. The web page consists of all important features of information available in the data base holdings of the particular archival Institution. The web page preparation is a skilled programme which can be done only by skilled programmers. In the case of Archival Institutions of India, the senior Archivists have to be trained in digitization and they have to prepare the content summaries of archival holdings.

The web site designers will prepare the web page programmes. Later that these pages should be available to the academics and the needy citizens for a fee. This will become one more source of income to the Archival Institutions of India in future. Reliable information venders would provide verifications such as the name of the data base, or service accessed, when it was last updated, and how the data is now available in complete shape. The reputation of the vendor in the profession is the guarantee provided to the buyer. The profiles of two leading companies of the U.S.A. who are professional online sources are given below:

1. American Business Information Inc- National Global scan- international, NJ. [New Jersy] Web site: http: www.ambest.com.
2. National Information Bureau Ltd., NJ.(New Jersy). Web site: http: www.nib.com.

The following are web sites relating to the archives of the U.S.A, and these are government departments:

A. National Archives & Record Administration [http:www.nara.gov]

B. State Archives, Michigan (http:www.SOS.state. mi.us/ history/archive\ht.ml)

C. http:www.archives.gov/index.ht.ml. U.S.NARA.

In this web site, categorized information under important headings like welcome, about research rooms, record management, record centers programmed, federal register, grants, exhibition halls, digital class room, presidential libraries, search sites index have been included.

The National Archives of Australia and many European countries have developed their web sites already and the web sites of Australia are available on the internet. One web site provides information on and links to archives and manuscript collections in Australia. Another one relates to the Australian Society of Archivists and the third one offers a gateway to archive resources of Australia while including indigenous, and federal resources, links, and on line displays.

Important web sites relating to Australia are as under:

[1] http: www.naa.gov.au/ [2] http: www. archivists.org.au/ [3] http: www.archieve.net.au/

The web sites developed by Canada and other European countries are mentioned below:

[1] National Archives Canada: http: www.archives.ca [2] Summit of the Americas-meeting on archives of 2001 held in Quebec city: http: www.Americas Canada. org/ events. Summit/ menu.e.asp.

National Archives of United Kingdom - [1] National

Archives of Scotland: http:www.nas.gov. uk. This is a Respitory of all public, legal and private archives. [2] Archives hub-national gate way to archives collections of United Kingdom ; http: www.archives. hub.ac.uk. [3] U.K. Data Archive- Specialist National Resource on social science and humanities; http: www. Data. Archive.ac.uk. [4] Public Record Office (PRO) : National Archives U.K holds 1000 years archival documents; http: www.pro.gov.uk

**National Archives, France:** Archives-Nationale: http: www.archives nationals.culture.gouv.fr/chan

**National Archives, Germany:** Master lists of Archives [1] http: www.tulane.edu./Imiller/master. html. [2] History Resources: http:www.princetomedu/ pressman/history.htm. search.

**National Archives, Spain:** [1] Archives in Spain: This web site provides links to a list of most important archives in Spain, http: www. ars virtual. Com/info/ enlaces.htm#arc.

[2] Archive General De Indias: Sevelle, Spain; this archives preserves the archival documents of Spanish colonies in West Indies, http:www.mcu.es/lab/ archivos/AGI.ht.ml.

[3] Archivo General De Simancas: Spain- Official site of the general archives of Fort Simancas in Spain located near the capital Madrid. Http: www.mcu.es/ leb/archives/ AGS.ht.ml[4] Archivo Historic National: Spain-Offical site of national historical archives in Spain. Features its history. A guide to access to its collections, http:www.mcu.es./ lab//Archivos/ AGN/ht.ml.

In addition to the above, United Nations has taken up a pioneering venture in the field of archives and computerization in the late 60'. The UNESCO has brought out a software package known as 'CDS\ISIS. This is an advanced non-numerical information storage retrieval software since 1985. To satisfy the need expressed by many institutions in developing countries. The package will help the institutions to streamline their information processing activities, by using modern technologies. This software relatively inexpensive, and was originally based on the main frame version of CDS\ISIS started earlier. While preparing the latest version, the UNESCO has taken advantage of several years of experience acquired in data based management and software development.

The main features of CDS\ISIS software are: [1] the handling of variable length of records, thus saving disc space, and store more information [2] a data base definition component allowing the user to define the data to be processed for a particular application, [3] a data entry component for entering data through user created data base specific work sheets, [4] and information retrieval component using a powerful search language, [5] a data interchange function [6] and many others. In the meetings and seminars held during 2001 for discussing this new software package only Librarians attended. Now, the UNESCO released a CD-Rom which includes CDS\ ISIS-Windows and the same is useful to Archival Institutions also. In the course conducted in Zimbabwe, the participants were given training for developing and acquiring skills so as to build and manipulate, maintain and manage non-numeric data bases using CDS\ISIS. In short, this is an information and retrieval software developed for information institutions, including archives especially in developing countries,to be able to streamline their information processing activities. [http:www.unesco. org\webworld\isis\index.ht.ml.]

[1] The UNESCO has also other on going projects useful to the archival institutions. The aims and objectives of these projects are as under:

[2] Encoded Archival Finding Aids, Development of Standard Tool on the international level. The project of the UNESCO\ICA will asses the possibilities of formulating recommendations for developing an international standard tool for encoding archival finding aids based on certain principles, [httprwww. unesco.org\ web-world\public-domain\projects\ eafa.ht.ml.]

[3] Guidelines for establishing digitization programmes in

libraries and archives. The guidelines are being developed by an trans-disciplinary team of library and archives experts and shall serve decision makers as well as library and archives managers particularly in developing countries, as a guide for planning digitization. [http:wwwunesco.org\web world\ public domain\projects\ digitizaion.html].

[4] Legal Evidence of Electronic Records-This project aims to assess the challenges posed by electronic records. [http:www.Unesco.org\webworld\public-domain\ projects\ evidences.html].

[5] Memory of World Programme-This programme aims to guard against collective amnesia calling upon the preservation of valuable archival holdings and library collections all over world ensuring their wide dissemination. [http:www.unesco.org\web world\ mdm\index2.html].

[6] Programme for the Preservation of the Audio and Visual Heritage- This programme provides basic information on the Unesco activities in the area of legislation, training, and publication etc., [http :www.unesco.org\ web world\ audio vis\ avarch.html].

Now it is an accepted fact that the use of public records is one of the fundamental rights of a democratic society. Public records are meant to be used for the benefit of the society. Many democratic countries have enacted laws ensuring the right to information to their citizens. Some of the countries which have enshrined this right in their constitutions are Finland [Official Documents act, 1951], the United States of America [Freedom of Information Act, 1956], France [1978], Australia [Freedom of information act, 1982], New Zealand [Official Information act, 1982], and India (The Right to Information Act, 2005) Canada [Access of information act, 1983] and India (The Right to Information Act, 2005).

Developing countries like India, with archival holdings of more than three centuries old and with the similar categories of archives in the State Archives departments also have to follow the example of the United States of America and other countries in the computerization of archives and develop web sites so that the information available in the archives of these departments of open period without restrictions will be useful to the administrators, scholars and to some extent to the common man in the coming years.

## CONCLUSION

Archives contain high destiny of virgin information which can be utilized by academics and citizens for variety of purposes. The citizens can use the archival sources to study how their elected representatives in panchayats, municipalities, legislatures, and parliament have carried out their responsibilities. This provides a sense of participation. As explained already in the preceding paragraphs, there are many benefits to the common man from the access to information. Information such as pertaining to citizenship, property, birth, marriage, death, court cases and any other sundry matters can be easily obtained without going to the government offices many times. This will ease out pressure on the day-to-day administration. There will be awareness among all sections of people about the value of public records or documents and their preservation on scientific lines for posterity. This gives social credibility and justification to the archival holdings both at the local and national levels.

## REFERENCES

1. Microsoft Internet Explorer- Links. International cooperation-UNESCO projects and programmes-html.
2. M.I.E. Archives U.S.A - collection. Search;.
3. M.I.E-M.S.N. search Australian archives.
4. M.I.E. Libraries and Archives, Span;.
5. M.I.E. Files of National Archives Record Administration. U.S.
6. M.I.E. yahoo search results for National Archives Canada. U.K. France. Germany.

# 9

# INDEX TRANSLATIONUM : A BIBLIOGRAPHICAL TOOL OF WORLDWIDE TRANSLATIONS

## INTRODUCTION

The conclusion of the treaty of Axi-la-chapel brought an end to the great war of 1914-1918. Besides the general destruction, the war wrecked many academic institutions and projects. Among such projects the *International Catalogue of Scientific Literature* (London) and among institutions the *International Institute of Bibliography* (Brussels) were to end their bibliographical activities. The League of Nations which was formed in 1920 after the war, felt the need for influencing 'the minds of men'. It soon formed the *International Committee for Intellectual Cooperation.* The Committee consisted of outstanding personalities such as Leon Bourgeois. Gilbert Murray, Henri Bergson, Albert Einstein, Marie Curie and R.A. Millikan. Based on the distinguished French writer, Paul Valery's concept *Societe des esprits* (an intellectual elite), the Institute International de co-operation Intellectualle was formed at the initiative of the French Government in 1925. The Institute strongly felt the need to emphasis the importance of books, bibliographical communication and control. Hence it spelt out the following programmes in its agenda besides other activities:

1. Dissemination of works of the mind by translation of literary master pieces by international bibliography and interlibrary loan.
2. The Institute to start the compilation and publication of *Index Bibliographics.*

## INDEX TRANSLATIONUM : THE EARLY YEARS

The *Index Translationum Reportire International des Traductions* was thus started by the Institute International de Co-operation Intellectualle during the momentous period between the two great wars in 1932 in the form of a quarterly bulletin. It was published from 1932 to 1940, till the beginning of the devastating second world war (1940-1945) This had ceased publication during the period January 1940 to June 1945. In the beginning it listed the translations published in six countries—Germany. Spain, UK, USA, France and Italy- The number of countries featured later in the *Index* had increased to 14.

Soon after the war the UNO was formed and the UNESCO was installed in Paris in 1946. The UNESCO took over all the projects and the staff which were left over by the Institute International de Co-operation Intellectualle. The *Index Translationum* was thus revived and started publishing for the second time in 1948 from 7-9 Place de Fontenoy 75700, Paris (France) which is its present headquarters. The reissued first volume contained 8570 entries from 28 countries including Brazil, Canada, Chile, Egypt and Turkey.

*Index Translationum* is an annual publication. Its text is both in English and French. Its current subscription rate is $75 per annum. The last volume printed on paper is volume 39 of 1993 which contained 60,543 entries from 56 countries. The Index changed from print to CD-ROM in 1993. Users can now take advantage of cumulative data built up since 1979, the year in which the *Index* was computerised. The 1998 volume contains almost one million entries from over 100 countries.

## SECTIONS OF THE INDEX

The *Index Translationum* has the following parts

1. Contents
2. Preface
3. Classification
4. System of arrangement of entries
5. Key to Abbreviations (languages)
6. Text of the bibliography arranged country-wise
7. Statistics of translations of the year country wise, and
8. Alphabetical list of principal authors.

## COLLECTION OF MATERIAL

National Libraries, National Commissions, Bureaus of Translations, Research Organisations and other organisations of the member countries of the UNESCO furnish the details of translation of works published in their countries. The *Index Translationum* volume of each year contains the translations published in the same year. But relatively a small number of translations published in earlier years not previously listed in the volumes of the earlier years are also published. The bibliographies of the translations are arranged under the names of the countries in French alphabetical order.

The *Index* covers every subject, including agriculture, architecture, art, biography, economics, education, geography, natural and social sciences, history, literature, management, medicine, philosophy, religion, science, technology, and sport. Almost 2,00,000 authors are listed and 400 languages are mentioned.

The information collected and furnished by the organisations for inclusion in the *Index* is a skillful work. It needs patient research and careful copying of the data and transliteration of titles of works, names of translation and other essential bibliographical information into Latin characters This is a tedious work but an essential and important task in a polyglot bibliography such as this work.

## TRANSLITERATION SYSTEM

The ISO system for transliterating Cyrillic alphabets used by the writers in the countries of Bulgaria, Byelorussia, Russia, Siberia, Ukraine and other East European countries has been employed in the Index in order to obtain uniformity in the spelling of the names of authors writing in those languages. In the case of other languages transliteration used is based on uniform international systems. Hence variant transliteration systems are used in this international index. This system is followed for the better and greater use of the *index* by the users in the different countries of the world.

## AUTHOR INDEX

At the end of each volume of the *Index* an alphabetical list of principal authors is given. This gives reference to translations by country codes and serial numbers. Preceding the author list, a statistical chart is given showing the number of entries against each country under the ten categories shown below. Finally the total entries'in the *Index* is given. This shows the translation activity in each country and also indicate the languages from which more translations are published. The statistical chart is an important one. It shows the strengths and weakness of translation activity in each country. Further it indicates the subject areas in which translations are more.

The analysis of translations listed in the *Index* for the last 50 years will reveal quite interesting things. The translation from the Indian languages into English and from English to Indian languages and also the translations between the Indian languages will reveal the flow of cultural influences from one language into another language. They also reveal the richness of the language from which translations are made.

The *Index* showed in the past that the *Bible* was largely translated work. Among the authors translated, Engles was on top for many years. During the days of Iron curtain, the Russian works were largely translated. The Russian Scientific Journals were translated from cover to cover in the UK and the USA. The contribution of India in the field of translations from English to Indian languages and between the Indian languages has been increasing year after year*.

## STRUCTURE OF THE INDEX TRANSLATIONUM

The bibliographical entries are arranged country wise. Within each national bibliography of translations, the entries are arranged alphabetically according to the ten main categories of the Universal Decimal Classification (UDC) scheme. These ten categories are listed as under:

0. Generalities, Bibliography, Information Science, etc.
1. Philosophy, Psychology
2. Religion, Theology
3. Social Sciences, Law, Education
4. Linguistics
5. Natural and Exact Sciences
6. Applied Sciences
7. Arts, Games, Sports
8. Literature (including books for children) and linguistic books as under category No. 4.
9. History, Geography, Biography (including memoirs and autobiographies)

The translated works under category 4, are not given under that category. They are shown under category 8. The

---

* The National Library, Kolkata provides entries for translations done in India. The Central Institute of Indian Languages(Mysore 570006) has developed a website Anukriti (www.anukriti.net)which among others provide list of translated works. —*Author*

listing of works of linguistics and literature are more useful to users if they are together under one category instead of listing them separately under the categories 4 and 8.

## SAMPLE OF ENTRIES

A sample of the text of the bibliography is given for better understanding of the bibliographical data provided for each entry. The sample shows the bibliographical entries of linguistics literature under the country name, India. This extract is taken from Volume 32. of the *Index Trannslationum* of 1972.

### An Illustrated Entry

**8 Litterature**

**Literature**

**Literatura**

355 Abbas, Khwaja Ahmad: Iru tuli nir [Tamj/Mukhtar/ Madras: Poompuhar, 1977. 174, HINDI *Do bund pani*

56 — Nanku nanparkal (Tam]/Mukhtar/Madras: Poompuhar, 1977. 120. ENG

57 — Oro putiyakalai pularntatu [Tam]/Mukhtar/Madras: Poompuhar, 1977. 218 ENG *Tomorrow is ours*

58 Advani, Kalyan Bulchand: Sah Latiph [Gujarati]/ Jayant Relvani/New Delhi: Sahitya Akadetni,.1978. 80. SINDHI

59 Agravala, Govinda: Nukati danam [Eng]/ Dvarkaprasad Lakhotiya/Churu: Smaskriti Shodh Sansthan, 1978. xvi, 101. RAJASTHANI

60 Ajavani, L.H.: Sindhi sahityana itihasna ruprekha [Gujarati]/Nalin Raval/NewDelhi: Sahitya Akademi, 1977. vii, 265. ENG

61 Akhllan: Citrapriya [Hindi] K.A. Jamuna/Delhi: Rajpal, 1978. 311. TAM *Cittirappavai*

62 — Cittirappavai [Malayalam]/C.A. Balan/Kottayam: D.C. Books, 1978. 408. TAM

63 — Flower of gold [Eng]/Vesta Hakim/New Delhi: Sterling Paperbacks, 1978. 163. TAM *Pon malar*

64 — Gopur ka dvip [Hindij/Sarasvati Ramnath/ AjmerKrishna Bros., 1978. vi, 121. TAM

65 Akhtar, Jamna Das: Amsu [Hindi]/Delhi: Ashok Pocket Books, 1978. 207. URDU *Ansu*

66 — Kasmir ki beti (Hindi]/Delhi: Ashok Pocket Books, 1978. 206. URDU

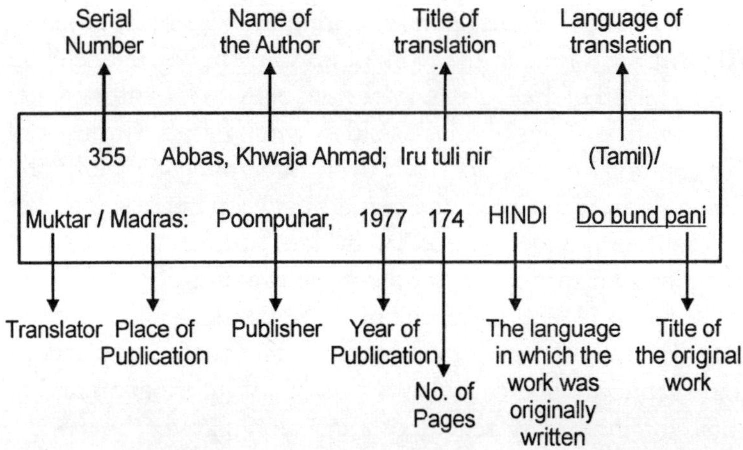


**Fig. 1. Showing the different parts of an entry**

An entry from the index is given above to illustrate each part of the entry.

In each entry information is provided about the original work and the translated work. The bibliographical information of the original works such as the place of publication, and year of publication, the publisher and the number of pages are not given. The information on preliminary pages and the size of the book are ignored.

The information received from different sources by the

office of the *Index Translationum* is closely examined to bring accuracy and uniformity in the entries. In the case of bibliographies forwarded without indication of categories and classification, the editor of the *Index* decides how to the specific works should be classified. The various national bibliographies are not always in agreement concerning the category of a specific work; Any confusion arising from lack of agreement in this respect may be overcome to a certain degree by consulting the alphabetical list of authors provided at the end of the volume.

## IMPACT OF THE INDEX

The *Index Translationum* during its existence of the last 70 years set a tone to the work of translation. Now translation is recognised globally as an important activity for international co-operation. Translation is as old as writing itself. Throughout the centuries translators have been attempting to bridge the cultures and break down the barriers between nations. It makes different language groups to understand each other and mitigate their frictions. After the establishment of the *Index* in 1932 many National Translation Centres, Bureaus and other organisations came into existence. A few such organisations and secondary source serials are listed for information and to show the increasing activity of translation all over the world.

1. *International Bibliographic by Ubersetzung/International Bibliography of translations* (compiled by) Heavy van Hoob. Pullah/Munchan, Verlag Documentation, 1973, XV, 591P.
2. National Translation Centre. *Consolidated index of translations into English*, New York, Special Library association, 1969, X, 948 P.
3. *Transdex Index.* Ohio, Bell & Howell 1974-Monthly
4. *World Index of Scientific Translations.* Delft, the European Translation centre, 1967-77. Quarterly, with annual cumulation.

5. *World transindex: announcing translations in all fields of science and technology.* Delft, International Translation Centre, 1978-v.l-Monthly.

The above are only few examples. In the *Ulrich* many serials of translations are listed.

## DIGITAL DATABASE

The *Index Translationum* has developed a digital database. It contains cumulative bibliographical information on books translated and published in different languages in about a hundred of the UNESCO's member states. The digital data of 1,300,000 translated works from 1979 in all disciplines, literatures, social sciences, natural and applied sciences, art, history etc., is available. The database is updated every quarter. Its website address is http.//www.unesco.org/culture/xtrEins/index. This information can be used by scholars and libraries through Internet connectivity. This provides ready made information about the translated works for translators who intend to translate any work from any language in the world. Thus, duplication of translation, the cost and time can be avoided.

## CONCLUSION

1. The *Index Translationum* is a comprehensive bibliography of translations of works published in the member states of the UNESCO. It is a first international effort for cultural diffusion between different language groups, nations and continents.
2. The information for assembling the *index* is furnished by the National Libraries, National Commissions, Bureaus and Academic Organisations. Hence the information in the Index is most reliable and authentic.
3. It is the most important source to find out the different works of each language translated into other languages in the world and provides access to their ideas and cultures overcoming the language barrier.

4. In view of its publication from 1932 onwards except for a few years of interruption during the second world war, the *Index* is an important bibliographical control tool in the field of translations.
5. For scholars who are not proficient in other world languages other than their own mother tongue it is a good tool to select books published in other countries and cultures and translated into their mother tongue for their reading.
6. It is also an important selection tool for libraries to build up their collections in the area of foreign literatures.
7. The *Index Translationum* helps to find out the different translations of a work. For example the *Ramayana* is translated into many languages of the world. The number of translations of a particular work is an indication of its importance as the citation of articles in Journals. It helps also to select a better translation out of the many translations of a work in a language.
8. Cover to cover translation of certain serials and books in science and technology helps the scientists and technologists to know the scientific discoveries and innovations in other languages and for their dissemination. This saves a lot of cost and time.
9. In polyglot countries like India, the *Index* is a very useful bibliographical tool to find out the translations from each national language into other national languages and the foreign languages.
10. Librarians, documentalists, researchers, publishers, journalists, translators, students, bookshops, all consult the *Index Translationum* into which the works are translated.]
11. The *Index* is the best reference tool for establishing statistics concerning translations allowing specialists to analyse international readership and publishing markets according to their needs.

12. The *Index* is a huge store house of information from which we can determine the trends in the tastes of the international reading public most frequently translated authors, and the influence of certain languages over others.
13. The annual output of translations in a country is a good barometer of its cultural level.
14. National library of each country should bring out a bibliography of translations into and from the national languages of their country for every 5 or 10 years. Such publications will be a good reference tool in academic and special libraries for the purpose of easy location and acquisition of important translated works.
15. The *Index Translationum* improved the awareness of translated works worldwide and thus provided a congenial environment for the suitable change of the minds of men from nationalism to internationalism.
16. Though there is still no universal bibliographical control for books and serials, the *Index* could achieve such control in the limited field of translated works, which should be taken as a model to achieve the UBC for books and serials too.

The *Index Translationum* has completed 60 years of its publication in 2008. It is the oldest publication of the UNESCO still continuing reflecting the ever growing translation activity world-wide. With the fall of empires and liberation of earlier colonies more and more member states are joining the United Nations and translation activity is increasing enormously. Enhanced levels of education, increased cultural exchange and the need, the desire to know and understand the other people, their culture, literature, art, science and civilisation contributed to the rapid growth of the *Index Translationum*. Its database in Paris is universally accessible through the Internet by scholars, translators and users. The *Index* is an example of par excellence for global bibliographical co-operation and control.

# 10

# Agricultural Information From Generation to Utilisation by Farmers in Rural India

## INTRODUCTION

India is one of the oldest civilizations with the rich cultural heritage. It covers an area of 32,87,263 Sq. kms. extending from the snow-covered Himalayas to Kanyakumari. It is seventh largest country in the world with a population of more than a billion, constituting 15 per cent of world's population. It is divided into 29 states, 6 Union Territories and 600 Districts. There are 3366 cities and towns and 5,57,137 villages or inhabitations. Nearly 70 percent of its population live in rural India. Agriculture and its related subjects are the major occupation of the people.

The agriculture sector, provides livelihood to about 64 per cent of the labour force, contributes nearly 26 per cent of Gross Domestic Product (GDP) and accounts for 18% share of the total value of the country's exports. It supplies large bulk of goods to the non-agricultural sector and industry. Thus the agriculture sector provides largest input to the country's economy. The agriculture sector covers different subjects such as land, crops both food grains and commercial crops, fertilizers, plant protection, horticulture, animal husbandry, poultry, dairy, fisheries, agriculture education, agricultural marketing and agricultural engineering. There are many other sub-facets to the above major ones which need information. Agriculture is a major industry in rural areas. After independence government took up to agricultural promotion programmes like. 'Green Revolution' which made India self sufficient in food grain production. The major crops grown are rice, wheat, jowar, bajra, maize, cotton, sugarcane, barley, gram, sesame and muster seeds. The growth of agricultural production from 1991-92 to 1999-2000 is shown in figure -1. Government, to carry out its national agricultural policy, established a number of supporting institutions both academic and research. Both at the centre and state levels, government created ministries, departments and institutions to support, monitor and supervise the agriculture programmes. It has the largest nexus to create awareness among the farmers through various channels and media.

Besides the Agricultural Universities and colleges there are many institutions and organizations, who generate agricultural information. There shall be linkage between the international agricultural information and national agricultural information systems.

## AGRICULTURAL INFORMATION

The agricultural information play's a key role on the farmer in deciding his agricultural activity. The source of information and its reliability are crucial in decision making. Communication of agricultural information to the farmers involves two stages: (*i*) Generation of Information; and (*ii*) Communication of Information.

**(*i*) Generation of Information** : The academic and

research institutions identify the problems relevant to farmers on various aspects of agriculture. These problems vary from region to region and crop to crop. These institutions take up both the individual and group problems and try to formulate solutions. While formulating the solutions, the existing information is used and new information is generated which is documented and communicated.

(*ii*) **Communication of Information** : Generated information will not have any value unless it is communicated to the farmers. The communication of information is done mainly through the following two channels: (*a*) Documents; and (*b*) Interpersonal communication.

(a) *Documents* : The documents are the major channels for communication of agricultural information. But in India problems such as widespread illiteracy and multilingualism impose a serious limitation on their effectiveness. Documentary sources are mainly useful to academicians and researchers rather than to practicing agriculturists.

(b) *Interpersonal Communication* : This is an effective source of communication to farmers. The government agencies, institutions and industries are making vigorous efforts to communicate agricultural information either through their own network or by organizing training programmes to farmers.

Due to lack of technical knowledge, the disseminated agricultural information is not understood properly by the farmers. This often results in their misguidance. For example, a trader, who is generally the most easily accessible person, tries to communicate the technical points such as use of insecticides, fertilizers, seeds, etc.in spite of the fact that he/she is not aware of the problems and their correct solutions. This results in

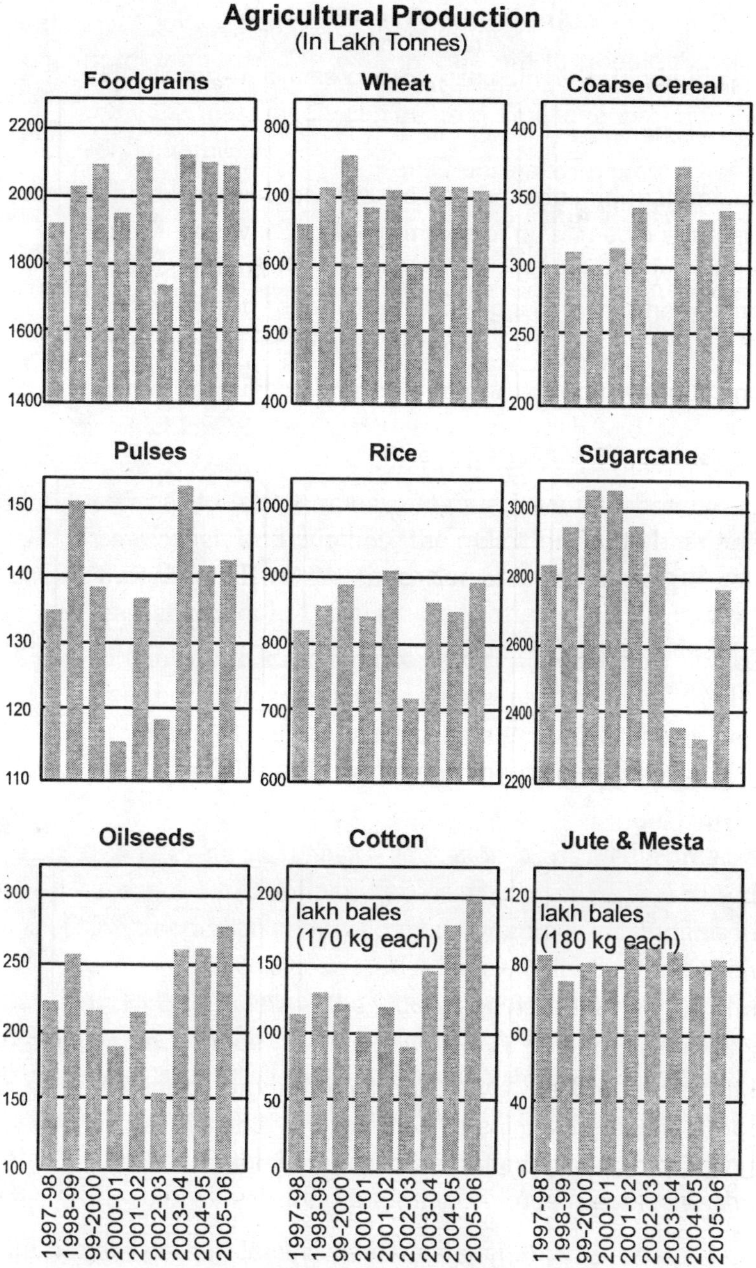


**Fig. 1. Growth of Agricultural Production**

disastrous situations. Figure 2 shows the schematic representation of the present flow of agricultural information to Indian farmers. (In the figure the abbreviation E.O. stands for Extension Officer and V.D./E.O. stands for Village Development/Extension Officer.)

The libraries are playing a very limited role in the flow of agricultural information to farmers. However, they are rendering a valuable service in the dissemination of agricultural information to researchers and scientists. The fellow farmers and their experiences too contribute a lot in the flow of agricultural information.

## DECISION MAKING

Communication of information puts the illiterate farmer into a state of confusion as the information is received by him through several channels and with a lot of modifications. Judging the relevance and accuracy of information is one of the vital tasks. This inevitably help the farmer in planning and programming of :

(a) Farming methods;

(b) Soil and crops;

(c) Inputs;

(d) Plant protection;

(e) Fertilizers, and

(f) Equipment,

The various aspects of communication such as language, form, style, and source of information will have an impact on the farmer. Also, there are several other factors that are involved in the decision making process by the farmers.

## GOVERNMENT AND AGRICULTURAL DEVELOPMENT

The Government had taken several steps to support the agricultural sector:

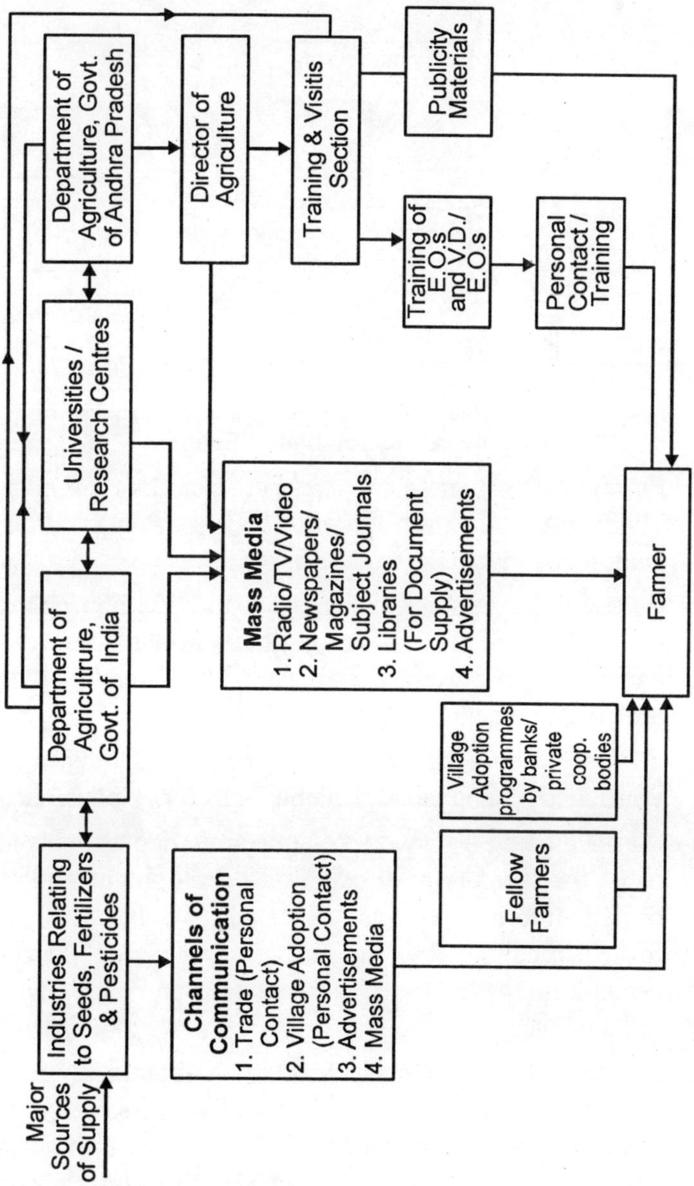


**Fig. 2. Schematic Diagram Showing the Present Flow of Agricultural Information to Indian Farmers**

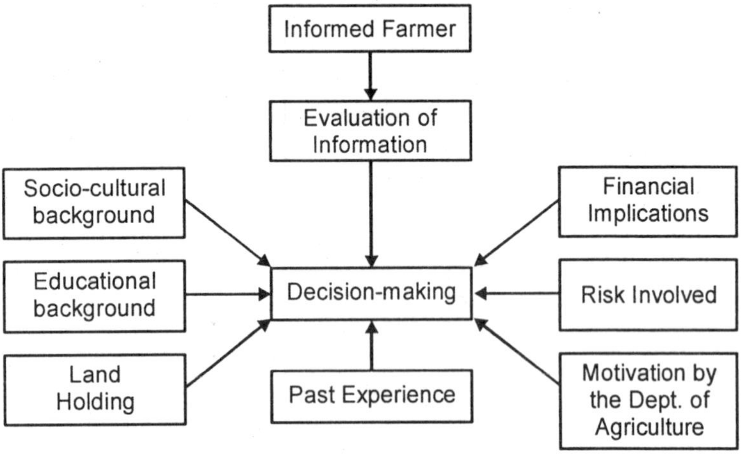


**Fig. 3. Factors involved in the Decision-making process of Agricultural Information in India**

i. By enacting several acts, (e.g., Fertilizer Control Order, 1983; Seed Control Order, 1983; See Act, 1966; Dangerous Machine Act, 1983, etc.)

ii. By establishing several institutions to provide information and training (e.g., Seed testing laboratories, improved Farmer's Agro-Service Centre; Farm Machinery Training and Testing Institute, etc.)

iii. By introducing different schemes, (e.g., Integrated Watershed Management Scheme; Soil conservation, etc.)

iv. By developing a network of agriculture departments to assist the farmers in agricultural development and to provide information required for taking right decisions, (e.g., Agriculture department offices at various levels, Agriculture extension personnel for interaction with farmers, etc.)

v. By establishing farmer's clubs to bring about changes in the agriculture sector. Farmer's clubs are expected to educate illiterate farmers so as to raise their awareness level. These clubs encourage diversification ofproduction pattern and help in right against unemployment through encouragement of farm employment. This scheme was introduced by the National Bank of Agricultural and Rural Development.

vi. By establishing academic institutions and supporting research.

vii. By subsidizing farm inputs and providing financial support in the form of loans.

All these programmes had definitely helped the farmers in increasing their agricultural output. But in spite of these programmes, a large number of farmers are not in a position to take advantage of the various agricultural development programmes launched by the Governments. This has been due to various barriers in the free flow of agricultural information. These are discussed in the following sections.

## INFORMATION COMMUNICATION

Information communication depends on two factors, namely, (*i*) Channels of information; and (*ii*) Barriers of communication.

**(i) Channels of Information :** The major channels for communication of agricultural information in India are:

- mass media;
- commercial and business establishments; and
- interpersonal/verbal communication.

Mass media such as TV, radio and newspapers have undertaken in a big way the task of communication of agricultural information. They have allotted specific time/space slots for this purpose. The periodicals, which are published in various languages, are engaged in the popularization of modern advanced agricultural techniques and practices. The pamphlets produced by the governmental agencies are not well organized in terms of information content. However, they are published in good number.

The commercial and business establishments such as

banks and industries have taken up village adoption programmes. Through these programmes, the sponsoring institutions provide all assistance including the services of a qualified technical expert for communication of the relevant agricultural information.

The interpersonal/verbal communication is an important channel of communication involving interaction of farmers with groups such as traders, fellow farmers and extension officers.

**2. Barriers of Communication :** The main barriers of communication are: Illiteracy; language (1652 languages are identified as mother tongue in India), terminology, inaccessibility to documentary sources, conservatism, irrational beliefs, traditions and social taboos, lack of sufficient number of qualified technical staff for bottlenecks in the free flow of agricultural information. However, it can be stated that lack of cohesive communication link hinders circulation of information. If the disseminated information is properly understood and used by the farmers, then it may result in increased agricultural output.

## OBSERVATIONS

- The existing agricultural information system does not meet the information needs of the farmers adequately.
- The various publicity materials being prepared by the Government fail to communicate the agricultural information properly.
- The agricultural extension personnel of the Governments are unable to cover all the areas falling in their jurisdiction as they have been burdened with the task of covering a large number of villages.
- Generally, the extension / development officers at the grassroot level, who have to transfer the agricultural information to the farmers, are not technically qualified.
- The traders, through their contact agencies and

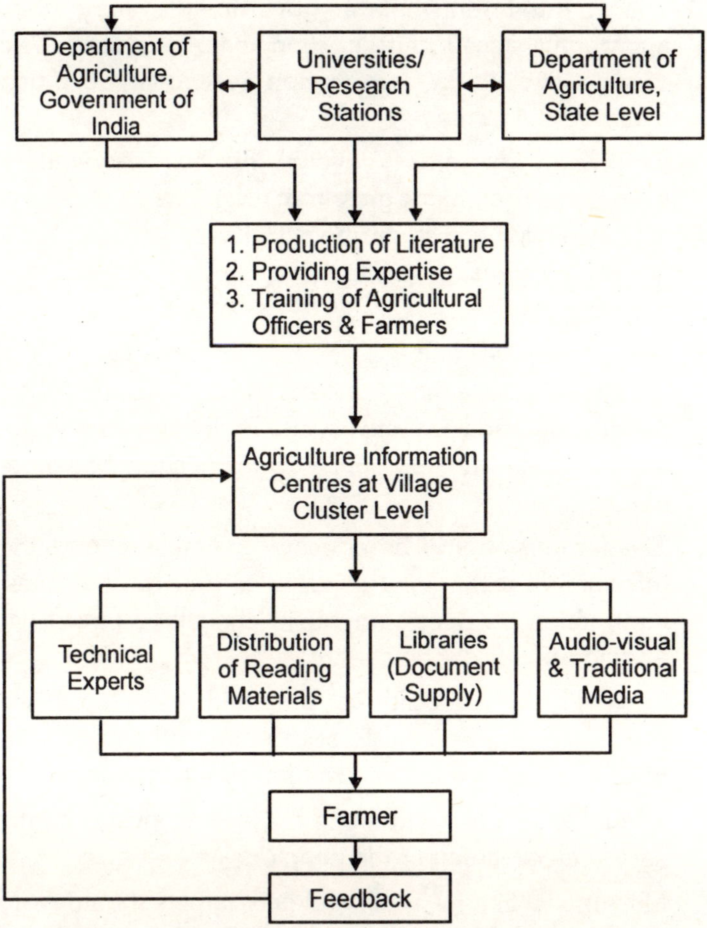


**Fig.4 Suggested Model for the Delivery of Agricultural Information to Farmers in India**

advertisements, are generally communicating only such information which suits to their commercial interest.

- The popular periodicals in local languages are insufficient.
- There is no proper coordination between the governmental and private agencies.
- The farmers, who are predominantly illiterate, are unable to evaluate the disseminated information in terms of its suitability, impact and relevance.

- The Central and State governments may take appropriate steps to further strengthen the system. The existing agricultural information system to be much nearer to the farmers.
- At present the areas covered by each agriculture extension person at the gross root level is wide. It doesn't enable him to be injctoseCjpntact with the farmers. More qualified extension personnel may be assigned the extension work.
- More intensive training should be provided to the extension personnel to understand the farmers, their psychology, traditions and beliefs. Their contacts with the farmers along with appropriate literature should be more frequent.
- The farmers should be educated to make use of the Information technology in order to find out the latest information on developments in agriculture both from abroad and inside the country.
- Local libraries should be provided with the latest brochures, posters charts both reading materials and visuals to disseminate information to the farmers.
- The information should be in the local language for the easy understanding of the people.
- Mass media like TV, radio and newspapers should carry more agriculture based programmes and news for easy and immediate flow of information to the rural communities.
- Computer facilities with INTERNET connectivity must be created in the village libraries for accessing information by the farmers.

## REFERENCES

1. BANNERJEE, S.R. and MOITRA.S "Agricultural Libraries in India *IN* GUPTA, B.M. etal (eds) Handbook of libraries,

Archives & Information Centres in India. Vol.1. New Delhi; Information Industry publications, 1984-85. pp 107-117.

2. INDIA. Ministry of Information and Broadcasting. India 2008; A Reference Annual. New Delhi; The Ministry, 2008.

3. HEMACHANDRA NAIDU, G and GUNJAL, S.R. "Agricultural Library and Information Services in India; growth, development and contribution of Agricultural University Libraries" *ILA Bulletin* 24:4, 1989.pp 186-193.

4. PHADNIS, S.P. and SHOAIB ASHAN, A. Indian Agricultural data and Information *Annals of Library Science and Documentation* 23:1, 1976.pp 31-48.

5. SHOAIB ASHAN, A and MEHLA, R.D. problems, needs and approaches of users to Information in agricultural sciences *ILA Bulletin* 22:3-4, 1986-87, pp 120-137.

# 11

# The Role of School Librarian as an Educator: An Overview

## INTRODUCTION

The Secondary Education Commission (1953: Chairman. A.L.Mudaliar, Govt. of India) in its report aptly remarked that "the aim of secondary education is to train the youth of the country to be good citizens who will be competent to play their part effectively in the social reconstruction and economic development of the country". The Commission further said that : 'it would require the services of a highly qualified and trained librarian who would be on par with other senior teachers in pay and school, a full-time librarian of this type'. The necessity of providing effective library services in schools to inculcate proper reading habits in the student community need not be overemphasized. The key to produce dedicated readers lie in the hands of the school librarian who would acquaint children with the range of books and other materials available and helping them.

## OBJECTIVES/FUNCTIONS OF THE SCHOOL LIBRARY

The main objectives of a school library include:-

(a) Offering opportunities to become more adept in the use of books and libraries.

(b) Provision of co-operative attitudes between the librarian and students, and

(c) Provision of increased and improved library service to the school community.

The more varied are the curricula in the school, the heavier are the demands on the library. The functions of a school are:

1. To teach a skillful use of books for self education.
2. To stimulate literary appreciation.
3. To demonstrate the desirability of books and libraries as companions of one's leisure.
4. To create an atmosphere conducive to the growth of reading habits.
5. Providing reading materials to the pupil for answering questions, doing assignments and solving problems.

A school library, thus, is an integral part of the school education. It supplements classroom teaching and is essential for the efficient functioning of every school.

## SCHOOL LIBRARIAN : ROLE, FUNCTIONS AND RESPONSIBILITIES

The school librarian acts as a friend, philosopher and guide to inculcate in the children:

— a love for reading and imbibe in them the spirit of continuously educating themselves to dispel their ignorance and other such factors

— to guide their energy into healthy, creative channels and stimulate their intellectual, educational and spiritual interest to elevate the individual

— infusing spirit of citizenship

— stimulating and educating public spirit and public morality.

The school librarian will have to impress upon the school administration to allot a period in the school time-table for each class to enable the students to use the library intelligently and diligently. An important task to the librarian is distribution of books and other materials among the children in the light of their tastes and interests, enabling the children to develop the reading habits, power of thinking and imagination; thereby leading the children to become library oriented. Multiple copies of good books of general interest must be made available by the librarian to the students to exploit the tendency of competition amongst the children. It is thus imperative that the selection of the right books to meet the needs of an individual child be taken note of.

The fourth law of library science as propounded by Dr.S.R.Ranganathan "Save the time of the reader" would be wholly justified by introduction of "open access" system in school libraries by the librarian. The Mudaliar Commission also recommends free access to books by the students.

If an effective school policy is formulated, then the library and librarian form an integral part of this. The importance and the central role of the librarian must be supported and accepted widely by the administration.

Since library skills and reading permeate so many areas of a child's personal and school life, the librarian has to carry his/her planning existing activities to other areas and agencies outside the school. These extend to local public libraries, community groups etc. The school librarian will involve himself in exploiting literary and information sources to the pupils, from the basic use of reference materials to the use of abstracts and on-line date bases. To support programmes on personal and educational counseling, the librarian, through co-operation of radio and television, should recommend to the administrator acquisition of books and other materials like charts, maps, portraits, audio-visual aids to meet the intellectual needs of the children.

Extra-curricular activities, essentially school based, the school librarian may involve himself actively as a part of imparting education include reading activities such as story telling (after school hours) which is an invaluable educational activity in any community, as and when done well, puts the librarian on top of its education.

Some of the extension activities that a school librarian must undertake to make students library minded include:

**1. Book exhibitions :** There should be a periodical exhibition of books in a school library which will draw the attention of the students to new books and materials. Students will be up-dated with latest information through such exhibitions.

**2. New additions :** To update the availability of books and other materials, new additions to the library should be brought out to the notice of the students.

**3. Film-shows :** This is an important audio-visual activity wherein by screening educative films and slides students will develop their academic intelligence and also fulfill the thirst of knowledge.

**4. Conducting student competition :** To inculcate a spirit of competitiveness amongst the students regular debates, essay writing etc., should be held in the schools, especially on important national days, birthdays of noted personalities, festivals etc. The school librarian will have to anchor the proceedings on such occasions.

**5. Bulletin boards :** School and library bulletin boards may, whenever necessary, display well-chosen clippings from newspapers and magazines, jackets of new books etc. to encourage visits to the library.

There is, however, no doubt that at bottom, the librarian's chief job is the "individual service" given to each of his young readers as they present themselves, backed by his knowledge of them and of the materials available for them to read and visualize. Thus the school librarian makes the library attractive to young readers by making it a center of children activity.The school librarian must be well-qualified (possessing a degree/ diploma in library science) and must be as much adept in child psychology and adolescent psychology as the teacher himself. In order to justify his profession, he must be familiar with children literature and capable of carrying out the technical organization of the library. Further he is expected to possess a wide variety of interests, vitality, personality, tact, enthusiasm to work with children as he does with adults. One of the important work of the school librarian would be to take care of the collection of the library which should be dynamically correlated with the changing curriculum. It is also important to note that the school librarian explain, in simple terms, the universally accepted Five laws of library science of Dr. Ranganathan to the children. He should train student volunteers to receive assistance in his day to day work, which in turn would enable students to get a chance to acquaint themselves with the technicalities of the library set-up.

Unlike in other developed countries, the school librarian in India would not get ample opportunities to make use of his professional qualities to the fullest extent since he is under the direct control of the authorities without any individual responsibility or powers.

A well equipped library helps in encouraging literary and cultural interest in students. But the position of school libraries in our country is not very satisfactory. A large number of schools, particularly primary schools, do not have a library at all. As many as 3,65,609 schools out of 6,34,144 are functioning without a library. Of these, majority of them are, of course, primary schools.

## CONCLUSION

The school library is the knowledge building laboratory where today's students are encouraged to practice thinking within a context of need, purpose and functional utility under the guidance of a competent librarian. A school librarian, given proper atmosphere and relevant powers, can help a child to create a reading habit somewhat along the lines of the old saying:

> "feed a man a fish and you feed him for the day" "Teach a man to fish and you feed him for life"

## REFERENCES

1. Bavakutty, M. 'Structure of school libraries' *Herald of Library Science*. 20: 3-4 (1981) p.230
2. India. Ministry of Education. Report of the Secondary Education Commission, Delhi, Manager of Publications, Govt. of India, 1953. Chairman: Dr.A.Lakshmanaswami Mudaliar.
3. Joseph, A.G. 'Developmental programme for elementary school libraries in India' *Herald of Library Science*. 24: 1-2 (1985) p.11
4. Kochhar, S.K. 'Library management : the school library' *Education Herald*. (March 16-31, 1987) p.29-31
5. Mukherjee, A.K. 'School library : some practical hints. New Delhi: National Council of Educational Research and Training, 1965.
6. Ramaiah, L.S. 'School libraries in India: an investment for national development' IN Academic libraries : Role in the national development , ed by Dorothy Isaac, A.A.N.Raju and L.S.Ramaiah. Madras: T.R. Publications, 1993. p.25-34.

# 12

# Rural Library Service in Andhra Pradesh

Man is by nature, inexorably inquisitive. Inquiry and doubt are the twin catalysts of progress. And yet, in the less developed countries grinding poverty, backwardness, illiteracy, superstition and obscurantism have proved a heavy damper on all developmental effort-physical and intellectual. The French writer Andre Maurios put it very aptly when he said:-

"A poor wretch who does not know where his next meal is coming from and who has no shelter from the cold and wet has no desire to improve his mind."

And again, Gandhiji sought to emphasise just this predicament of the average Indian when he observed –

"The human bird under the Indian sky gets up weaker than when he pretended to retire. For the millions it is a vigil or an eternal trance. The hungry millions ask for one poem– invigorating food".

In this backdrop, therefore all effort at development will have to be intergrated with the struggle for survival of the Indian masses.

Any cognisable success of such efforts at improving the quality of life of the community as a whole depends, in the main, on the participation of all sections of the people. The informed, spontanepus and, willing participation of the people is directly related to their social awareness which in turn is determined by the quality of education available to them. Development is accordingly to be recognised as a well co-ordinated, multidimensional effort with education as the cutting edge.

Attempt at educating the masses as conceived today begins from a fallacious premises.The masses are assumed to be wholly ignorant and "unintelligent". They may be unlettered and less sophisticated, but they are endowed with considerable amount of uncanny, native, intelligence which certainly helps them to discern and discriminate the good from the bad, the desirable from the undersignable. It is these reserves of native intelligence which have to be drawn out, provoked, promoted and utilised to help them to educate themselves. We will perceive this once we identify ourselves with them. The assignment calls for sympathy, dogged determination, dedication, tender care and perseverance. Such education has to be continuous and consistent. And the only agency which could provide service, informed by the aforesaid qualities, is the library.

## PRESENT SCENE

With the advent of library legislation, first in 1948 in Chennai and later in 1960 in Andhra Pradesh, attempts were made to organise library service to the rural masses. Today we have 24 district libraries, 790 branch libraries, 199 village libraries 602 Book Deposit Centres. In addition, it is reported that book packages are distributed in villages by cycle rickshaws, carts and so on. Many of these, as we know, are urban oriented, their services limited to recreational reading and a semblance of skeletal extension services. The departmental report (Libraries Department, A.P : Administration Report 1980-81) proclaims that of these several libraries 521 branch libraries are located in rural areas.

Together, with the 199 village libraries, 1540 libraries stated to be managed by Grampanchayats, – We presume these are located in big sized villages and about 400 aided libraries, they add up to around 2700 libraries, which apparently claim to cater to the information needs of the rural masses. In Andhra Pradesh we have 27,221 villages. Even if one third of them are considered small hamlets with less than 1000 inhabitants per hamlet and hence cannot constitute a basis for viable service centres, there are about 18,000 villages which are not covered by any service. Against this, existing library service only 2700 villages leaving more than 15,000 villages without any service. And taking into consideration the fact that about 8 crore (census 1981) people of the state live in the villages and only 40% (average) are literate-rural literacy should be even less existing services cover only about 3.2 crore, people, knowing as we do that even these village libraries do not possess representative book stock and attend to only recreational reading and that again restricted to about 40-50% of the village's literates, it does not call for any extraordinary intellectual exercise to realise how woefully inadequate the library services are. The problem is further compounded by the fact that our schools-primary and secondary in the rural areas do not have any libraries. State funding for library service – in schools and public libraries as a complimentary educational service comes in driblets and even scarcer is the conviction, perspective and vision to utilise the library as a centre of creativity and catalyst for social change.

It is relevant to recall that the review committee on libraries (1976) headed by Justice Sri Gopal Rao Ekbote lists out some basic fundamental lapses in the services organised by the State Library System. (See Appendix I : An extract from Vavilala's Report).

Also, the provision of section 14 of the A.P. Libraries Act, 1960 have not been respected in that no district plans or state level plan had been drafted for implementation. Thus the foregoing scene shows a lack of will, even less of a sense of direction and above all a lack of commitment to philosophy of library as a purprosive agency of life-long, continuing education. Even the few useful changes recommended by the Review Committee (1976) have not been taken up for effective implementation till date. Thereafter, the entire system plunged into the vortex of inflation, increasing costs and dwindling resources compounded by astounding indifference of the authorities which led the library system to a grainding halt in terms of establishment of new libraries, acquisition of new books in existing libraries, less co-ordination and even less service, library service from these on settling down to a humdrum routine.

## VAVILALA REPORT

In the wake of the services in the existing centres proving ineffective and arising directly out of the observations of Ekbote Committee on the role of place of private (subscription) libraries, came the vavilala committee report recommending that the spontaneous establishment of a large number of private reading rooms and libraries by enthusiastic groups in the state should be encouraged creating a climate conducive to promotion of the reading habit and linking them up with large scale literacy drive with substantial aid coming from government towards their effective organisation and maintenance. The committee stressed on urgent need for local initiative in extending library service to larger sections of our people, more in the rural areas. Government accepted the scheme in principle and issued orders. There after no scheme was evolved and no efforts made to implement the government's decision on the committee's recommendations.

### Raja Ram Mohun Roy Library Foundation

In the year 1972 the Foundation was set up with the immediate primary objective, among others :

— "Of quantitative expansions of library service, particular in the non-metropolitan areas with a view to developing reading habit among the people."

— This objective was further amplified by the Foundation's first chairman Prof. Nurul Hasan when he said :

— "The foundation will make special efforts to ensure that new libraries are set up in all districts where they do not exist and the district libraries are enabled to service a chain of libraries in the rural areas so that these come within the reach of the common people."

Under the scheme an amount of Rs. 4 lakhs annually (Rs. 2 lakhs states contribution plus Rs. 2 lakhs foundation's contribution) is placed at the disposal of the A.P. State Library Planning Committee of the foundation with the Director of Public Libraries as convenor for purchase and distribution of books to rural libraries. Beyond this no other promotional activity has been taken up. By some strange alchemy the work of selection and distribution is entrusted to the state level committee for book selection for the Zilla Grandhalaya Samastha libraries in Andhra Pradesh. The working of the scheme suffers from the following short comings which appear to strike at the very root of the primary objective of the foundation referred of the primary objectives of the foundation referred to above.

1. A review of the method of selection of books and the libraries identified for distribution of these books shows that an over whelmingly large majority of books are distributed to the State Central Library, State Regional Libraries and District Central Libraries only which serve non-rural areas and which have separate Government funding facilities.
2. Branch Libraries which are starved of funds in many cases are thus denied those books.
3. Large scale avoidable duplication of titles year after year is noticed resulting in wastage of scarce resources.

4. No machanism is available to check such duplication.
5. The committee meets hardly more than once or twice in a year so that by the time a title is approved by the committee for distribution, more often than not, it disappears from the market.
6. Selection itself is erratic and arbitrary in the sense that.
   (a) Copies of same title (abridged or otherwise) published by two or more different publishers with different price tags but same content are listed out for purchase and distribution.
   (b) Truncated sets of a multi-volumed book or book of multiple parts are picked up for distribution at different points of time rendering the sets useless and resulting again in wastage of resources.
   (c) Popular science, mathematics and social science books selected for one group of libraries are denied to another group.
   (d) Old classical fiction titles in differnt languages are invariably found in the lists approved year after year. Infact, classical fiction is invariably acquired when a new library is established. Therefore distribution of classics (Fiction) again and again only results in duplication and wastage of resources, and so on.

What with the several acts of ommission and commission of the authorities/committees, the foundation's basic objective has been undermined and service to the rural masses is the casuality. No wonder, then, that libraries and their services do not appear to be relevant to them. From what is detailed above it should be evident that there is a complete paralysis of the system.

In the society outside values like voluntarism, sacrifice and an urge and ache to be useful to society have faded out. Carrersim, opportunism, monetarism have surfaced in a big way. Personal advancement has eclipsed community interests.

The conciousness that man for his manifold needs and wants is indebted to society and is obliged to redeem this social debt is violently put down. Individual accumulation at the cost of the rest in society is acclaimed as achievement. This has made deep inroads to tarnish the personality of rural India. Therefore, is a sea-change. We are today caught in the coils of the trauma of violent cultural decimation.

If we are to be true to our profession we have to immediately move away on to a different track, attempt to readopt those cherished, abiding values, recapture the rythm of concerted action of the early years of the library movement in the state, to rededicate and to re-educate.

## New Orientation

The library is now to be recast; into a vibrant instrument of continuing education. It can take on this new role only if its services can be organised to make a more meaningful impact in the daily life of different sections of the rural community, viz. the artisan, .draftsman and the labourer, the farmer, the industrial enterpreneur, the students, the women and youth, the unlettered and neo-literate and so on, in addition to the usual service of recreational reading. This arouse the inherent inquisitiveness of the. yillager and hold it on, a small beginning could be made by reviving the old practice of reading out the newspaper columns and important articles from select journals for the benefit of the unlettered in the village. This proved so successful in the days of the National Liberation Struggle.

**Students and Youth :** In the background of a large number of poor households having barely a single room it is impossible for students to find a quiet place at home to sit and study. This gap can be filled - in by the library in providing for a separate room and a separate collection of books for students in the village to pursue their studies undisturbed. This will give them the additional advantage of the availability of a few reference books in the immediate vicinity. This should be done in addition to the normal extension activities like lectures, symposia, seminars, birthday celebrations of local celebrities, elocution and essay writing competitions. Such an approach will help them to acquire the habit of extended reading, select and sift out essential data and material and finally to extend the horizon of their comprehension.

**Women :** Literacy among women in general is low. With rural women it is even more less. Special care has, therefore, to be bestowed on programmes of this group. Programmes have to be devised primarily to highlight, and educate them on problems like equal rights with men, social emancipation of women, the dowry evil, additional employment opportunities including self employment opportunities and special training facilities available in the area etc., in collaboration with local women's organisation. All relevant literature should be acquired and made available. Audiovisual material should be freely made use of in these programmes.

### Craftsmen and Artisans

Many of them may be illiterate. A large number of them are poor and are hard but to in eking out a livelihood. They could be attracted to the library if its services, in addition to the usual could concentrate on providing information on alternatives in respect of (*i*) Sources of raw materials, (*ii*) marketing facilities which could fetch them some marginal additional profit, (*iii*) transportation facilities, (*iv*) bank (cooperatives or otherwise) credit facilities, (*v*) new and improved technology suited to their crafts and arts, (*vi*) improved machinery and tools which would save time and labour, presently spent on their job and (*vii*) opportunities for diversification into ancilliary units and so on. For these to make a serious and effective thrust, audio-visual material like film strips, casettes etc., should be freely utilised.

### Farmer

A considerable amount of effort is already being made

by the agriculture department and allied departments. The information output of these could be collected and provided in addition to encouraging formation of local discussion groups in collaborations with these and other departments and other voluntary organisations. It should be the endeavour of the library to make the farmer feel at home on the premises and see for himself that all the information relevant to his vocation is available in one place without his having to run about from office to office. Every appreciable achievement by local farmers should be highlighted and publicised to enable them and their group to get the feeling that society needs them and cares for them.

**Labourer**

The feeling that their basic needs are ignored is the strongest in this group. All relevant literature in respect of housing facilities and future programmes, drinking water facilities, changes, sanitary arrangements, prevailing wage structure and opportunities for additional facilities and lastly all provided to them in large measure through audio-visual equipment. Since a majority of them are unlettered, information regarding educational opportunities available to them including adult educational facilities should be presented to them in a more attractive fashion.

**Entrepreneur**

As in the case of the craftmen and artisans the local entrepreneur should get the benefit of better choice if he is given information regarding alternatives of (*i*) sources of raw material, (*ii*) market facilities (*iii*) transportation, (*iv*) bank credit facilities, (*v*) new and improved technology, (*vi*) machinery and tools (*vii*) setting up ancilliary industries etc., The entrepreneur and the local community would then be in position to recognise the library as a source of vital importance. In all these services the library should make to collect and disseminate related literature put out by the several government, quasi government agencies, learned societies and voluntary agencies etc.,

Free use should be made of audio-visual aids in all these sectors. In acquiring such aids, national agencies like the Raja Ram Mohun Roy Library Foundation etc., the central and state governments, should be requested to set apart funds for the purpose, since education and library facilities for rural areas are avowedly their basic commitment.

## Adult Education

The Central and State Governments have undertaken a massive adult education programme involving about Rs. 800-1000 crores in the Plans. But the programme as adopted does not seem to identify the library at the village or other level as capable of any significant role. For a moment, it looks as if the effective part played by libraries during the National Liberation struggle in organising adult education is forgotten. The village library, to begin with, should acquire and provide all adult education literature and literature for neoliterates to the unlettered in the villages, co-ordinate activities of voluntary agencies in the field and help in imparting a meaningful thrust for programmes involving education for the unlettered.

## Mobile Libraries

The importance of mobile libraries cannot be over emphasised. They bring the books to the door step. They are used extensively by women, children, senior citizens and the physically challenged who cannot afford to go to the local library premises.

## Library Tours

Organised groups of dedicated library workers will once again have to undertake extensive tours in the interior villages carrying the message of rejuvenating the rural scene through purposeful library service as in the 1920's and 1930's and recapture the old enthusiasm that distinguished the library movement.

## Voluntary Associations

Voluntary associations normally are recognised and are expected to function in a democracy, as the eyes and the ears of the community. With the advent of the Library Act and the creation of Zilla Grandhalaya Samasthas and the Directorate of Public Libraries, not only have the voluntary associations come to be ignored but their role in promotting a more congenial library climate and their work, both in the present and in the past, is getting undermined. Even apart from this, while libraries and services have basically to function for the people and among the people at large, the department and the Zilla Grandhalaya Samasthas function in cloistered halls and behind the closed doors. Every scrap of paper is a 'Classified document' not accessible to the public and voluntary organisations. To cite but one example the so called 'Master Plan' for development of libraries in the state finalised some 15 years back is a closed book to the public. It should in all fairness has to be made available to the public and associations for wider discussion both for an understanding of the plan and eliciting suggestions for amendents and modifications from all those who are familiar with the local situations. It is not as if all the wisdom in the world is concentrated in the few who drafted/approved it. No one today, knows anything about its content. It has accumulated dust today for all we care. While all these agencies are maintained with public funds, but their activities and reports thereon are scrupulously kept away from the public.

While associations have been downgraded by the authorities some of them have themselves grown moribund. Others have gone adventurous, championing irrelevant issues, some others, again, have been distorted and disoriented to suit personal ambitions. A few have drifted to function within narrow grooves and self imposed barriers. All of them appear to have shied away from the people. It is time for all to review their respective roles, realise the basic duty to the people and redraw their priorities so that they could reflect people's aspirations, project their personality of the people and the state.

## Funding

The finances presently made available to library services in the state are scarcely propertional to the responsibilities in terms of services to be rendered. The few basic changes suggested above involve sizeable investment in library service which is unavoidable and essential if we wish the present drift to decadence to be. reversed. It is time that we realised that this funding is an investment in development of human resources, investment for a stronger, more alert nation an investment in the future. Withholding funds, for this would mean not only hurting the future of the community but also a wastage of all that was over the decadas invested in formal education because those that out of schools and colleges are bound to lapse into relative illiteracy if they are not supported by adequate library services during the rest of their life. It would also mean that we set at naught the solemn pledge we made to people- in article 41 of the Constitution about their right to education.

Let us, therefore, pledge to rededicate ourselves to this cause and work as sincerely, honestly and devotedly as the earlier doyens like, Ayyanki, Suri Vankata Norasimha Sastry, Gadicharla Hari Sarvothama Rao, Bhupatiraju Thirupathiraju, Madapati .Hanumantha Rao, Suravaram, Pratapa Reddy and host of others who spent their lives in working for this cause. Let us take courage to respond to Gurudev Tagore's call

"Where the mind is without fear and head is held high;

Where knowledge is free;

Where words come out from the depth of truth;

Where tireless striving stretches its arms towards perfection;

Where the clear stream of reason has not lost its way into the dreary desart sand of dead habit;

Into that heaven of freedom, my father, let my country awake."

## APPENDIX-1

[Extract from varila Gopalakrishaiah's Report on Private Libraries].

"It is well known that private efforts in organising libraries have been enormous". In fact they were the pioneers of the library movement. There are libraries which are more than 75 years old in the state. Some of the libraries have very ancient and rich collections of books and manuscripts, Some of them however are languishing because of lack of funds and proper administration while some others are torn with feuds and dissensions. All of them have reading rooms with periodicals and newspapers. Large number of people are found to be attending these private libraries which are scattered all over the state. Then there are other libraries which are registered but do not *get* any grant from the Government or the Zilla Grandhalaya Samsthas. There are yet a large number of libraries which are neither registered with the Department nor are getting any grant from any where.

The number roughly estimated of such libraries in the state is put at 6,000. There are however no means to verify the same. A survey ought to be made not only about their number but also the areas they cover by providing service. There is no specific material available to indicate what stock of books all these libraries possess and to what extent they serve the people through newspapers and periodicals. This very important aspect of the library service has been completely ignored till to-day. The limited service which the departmental libraries are rendering makes the presence of these institutional libraries very essential. Foresight is a scarce commodity even at the present day. It is generally assumed by the Zilla Grandhalaya Samsthas and their libraries that their obligation is limited to their libraries. They do not feel in any manner responsible either for organising a system including these institutional libraries of trying to find out their problems and the sources to meet it them. That is the reason why the. Zilla Gyandhalaya Samsthas never took cognizance of such institutional private libraries. It is necessary to bring all these private libraries into the fold of the state library system. It would be disastrous to keep these private libraries outside the system.

1. "The rules envisage a scheme that is to say, a plan to be prepared by each district..., there is no master plan of any district and consequently there is no state plan;
2. The classification and cataloguing is not attended to properly .... has not been completed in most of the libraries. The State Central Library is doing precious little in this regard .... (This lapse) could not be satisfactorily explained by any of the District Librarians;
3. The importance of bibliography (compiling one for Telugu books etc.; is perhaps not realised by those who are concerned with it.....) After some initial efforts, the attempt seems to have at least for the present been kept in abeyance. Nobody seams to be interested in preparing bibliography for the period prior to 1958 or subsequent to 1963 and upto date;
4. Compilation of Union Catelogue of Telugu books is under preparation. It has taken several years. The position is that the state has no Union Catalogue
5. The development of the State Central Library and that of the Regional Libraries has not been on proper lines;
6. The linking of the libraries has been found to be inadequate in more than one respect;
7. There are many private libraries. Some of them are very ancient and possess rare books and manuscripts. In the absence of proper interest being taken by the Department and the people concerned, most of the ancient libraries are languishing. Private libraries have not been afforded

their legitimate place in the state library system;

8. It would be disastrous for the State Library system to keep those private libraries outside the systems;
9. Library co-operation or inter-library loan is not organised on modern lines..... Existing practice is not adequate; and
10. In the present organisational structure of libraries there are no effective linkages between the Regional Libraries and the State Central Library and between Zilla Grandhalaya Samasthas and the Regional Libraries".

# 13

# Loss of Books in Libraries and Remedial Measures

## INTRODUCTION

The concept of library service has undergone changes in course of time. It is no longer regarded as a storehouse of books but as a service unit to provide information and documents to meet varying requirements. As a sequel to this change in perceptions, the library collections tend to be thrown open to the users to enable them to have direct access to any document for consultation. Thus, from the old method of tying documents to shelves, a new system of making them available to the maximum users for maximum utilization has emerged. *Open access system as it is known, has its own share of drawbacks, one of which is the larger no of documents being lost from library*. Illegal removal of documents from libraries is a universal phenomenon registering wide variations from country to country based on its socio-economic and cultural milieu. Books are removed for varying purposes: *out of bad habit, as a business proposal* (in case of manuscripts and rare books) *and for meeting immediate Informational requirements.*

Proper security measures and checking, and other promotional approaches can drastically check this trend.

It is necessary to examine all aspects of the problem of loss of books faced by libraries and to suggest a common set of elementary security steps which could be taken to make sure that books are not easily removed and, if they are removed, there should be some process of accountability.

## NORMS ON LOSS OF BOOKS

The first attempt in India to determine an upper limit of permissible loss in libraries was made by the *University Grants Commission (1959) through its Library Committee headed by S.R. Ranganathan*. It recommended loss of two volumes per thousand volumes issued in an open access library, as permissible limit. This decision was resented by some working librarians, especally of acadamic libraries. Perhaps it might have prompted S.R. Ranganathan to change his stand on the issue inside a year. It is reflected in *the 2nd edition of Library Manual (1960)* where in he preferred the upper limit of permissible loss at three volumes per thousand volumes issued in an open library.

After lapse of a long time this issue came up before another UGC Committee *viz. the Committee on Procedure etc. of Stock Verification in Central University libraries in 1969*. J.S. Sharma, a university librarian and a member of the Committee vehementally advocated for loss of five volumes per thousand volumes circulated/consulted as permissible limit. The Committee, however, postponed a decision on this issue on the plea that the data pertaining to quantum of loss in various libraries be made available first. The desired data was not collected and the old norm of the UGC viz., two per thousand volumes issued in an open access library as permissible loss continued.

The *Indian Library Association since 1969 held the view that loss of four volumes per thousand volumes circulated/*

*consulted in a library be accepted as permissible ceilling. The Rajasthan College Principals' Conference, Bilwara (1969) recommended six per thousand volumes issued* as authorised loss. The *Gujarat Granthalaya Sewa Sangha state library association, was for the upper limit of seven volumes per thousand volumes issued in a library.* There are also instances of librarians pleading for fixing the upper limit as a percentage of the total annual stock of a library. This approach, however, failed to muster support from other working librarians, who held the view that the norms of inevitable loss should be based on the use of library materials and not on their total stock. Thus, the upper limit of inevitable loss in library as has been widely suggested by library professionals is between four and seven volumes per thousand volumes circulated/consulted in a library, which differs substantially with the upper limit decided by the UGC Library Committee in the year 1959(vide Appendix-1).

The Agricultural Libraries Survey and Study Team (1973) had recommended 5/1,000 publications for writing off. These recommendations were reported to be based on the Ramaiah Committee (1969) recommendations that *in the open access libraries the loss of the five books for every 1,000 books consulted and/or issued out on loan should be considered a reasonable loss and should be written of.* This is believed to be quite liberal compared to the norm followed in European libraries, where loss of two or three publications per thousand is considered very high.

The Ministry of Finance, Government of India vide GFR 116 stipulates that loss of three volumes per one thousand volumes issued/consulted in a year may be taken as reasonable provided such loss *cannot be attributed to dishonesty or negl igence on the part of the librarian concerned. Loss of book of the value exceeding Rs. 200* (Rupees two hundred only) and *books of special nature and rarity shall invariably be investigated and consequential action taken.* All *such losses will, however, be written off only by a competent authority.* (Vide Appendix-2).

## DETECTING THE LOSS

Stock verification is the universally accepted tool of discovering the items which are missing. Stock verification is a much sensitive and controversial issue in library collection management. The most prominent complaint against stock verification is *the fear of being beaten by the stick which they prepare in the shape of findings of stock verification.* Other reasons are *cost factors, shortage of staff, lack of time, disruption of library work and service etc.* In case sufficient resources are made available in the library and if authorities follow an enlightened direction in the disposal of losses, the resistance of library staff to stock verification may disappear.

Though some advanced countries have given up the practice of stock verification, it is still continued in India in consideration of the existing conditions. The universities prefer a system under which stock verification is a continuous process and is organised in such a way that it forms part of the daily routine of library work. A very large library like the National Library, Kolkata has a separate stock verification division whose sole duty is verification of books. Some states also follow this method in its various public libraries.

The libraries under the Government of India and libraries of state governments, by and large, follow the *General Financial Rules of the Government of India*. Third Estimates Committee (1965-66) of Lok Sabha took a serious view on Maulana Azad Library of Aligarh Muslim University for not verifying its stock and made a strong recommendation that at least once in two years the stock should be accounted for so that ways and means could be found to avoid loss and pilferage of books.

The latest directives from the Government of India are contained in *Ministry of Finance, Department of Expenditure Office Memorandum No. F 23(7)-E.II(A)/83 dated 7.2.1984* which provides; ...(v) *Complete annual physical verification of books should be done every year in case of libraries having not more than 20,000 volumes and not fewer than two library qualified staff. In case there is only one qualified staff, the verification may be done as per sub-para(vi). (vi) Complete physical verification at intervals of not more than three years should be done in. the case of libraries having more than 20,000 but not more than 50,000 volumes.*

(vii) *Sample physical verification at intervals of not more than five years may be done in the case of libraries having more than 50,000 volumes. If such a sample verification reveals unusual or unreasonable shortage, complete verification shall be done.* (*Vide* Appendix-2).

## ACCOUNTABILITY OF LIBRARIANS AND THEIR STAFF

Holding librarians/staff responsible for loss of books and recovering loss from their salary has always been a major irritant to the library professionals. It is not only considered as *a mark of disrespect* to them but *also is against the law of the land and principles of natural justice*. Unless there are concrete proofs of dereliction of duty or misconduct (leading to loss of books) one is not expected to be penalised. In the case of some libraries, the decision to recover is taken unilaterally without seeking an explanation from the librarians/staff, though the authorities concerned are aware that they have neither removed books nor have allowed the same. Besides, in the context of open access system., the chances of loss of documents have increased manifold. The over enthusiasm to eliminate library loss in this fashion-may ultimately reflect in reduced use of library, it is feared.

This line of thought has led to the recognition of the concept of *inevitability of loss* of items from the library which is now acknowledged in all parts of the world. The Ranganathan Committee conceded this stating, *even with the best of safeguards, the most human treatment possible and vigilance of a high order, there will be some loss. The authorities of a library should be prepared for it.*

This frame of reasoning has been found prevalent in later thoughts and reports like the Advisory Committee for Libraries (Sinha Committee), Govt. of India, 1959, the National Policy on Library and Information Systems A Presentation and the UGC Committee on Procedure etc of Stock Verification in Central University Libraries, However, an exception is the case of Government of Tamil Nadu which has kept a controversial provision for recovery of cost of lost books from the staff (Vide Appendix-3). The National Policy on Library and Information System: A Presentation states that *the user should be allowed as free and unrestricted access to library resources as possible and in doing so losses of documents may occur. Such losses should be guarded against as best a. library can, but ultimately, the .. librarian should not be held responsible for the losses which could not be avoided.* The Sinha Committee in this context stated, *we have no hesitation in saying that such practices are iniquitous and unheard of in the library practice of any advanced country in the world. In the first place, the safety of library books depends on the moral tune of its users and no librarian, unless he is to restrict severely the, use of books, can prevent the depredations of unsocial elements. Secondly since no librarian is adequately paid, the effect of asking him to pay f.or the loss of books would be that he' will place all books in his charge under lock and key and this nullifies the fundamentals of a good public library.*

Shri J.S. Sharma, a member of the UGC Committee on Procedure etc. of Stock Verification in Central University Libraries suggested in a note that *the responsibility of the losses, which if inevitable in open shelf system and in view of the social and economic conditions prevailing in our society, should not be fixed on the librarian and his staff.* The General Financial Rules of the Government of India also reflects the same spirit as its has allowed loss of three volumes per one thousand volumes issued/consulted in a year provided such loss could not be attributed to dishonesty or negligence on the part of the librarian and the staff.

Nanda. U. B and Goyal. S. P in a paper persented in the 29th All India Library Conference notes that the *Loss of books in the libraries is an inevitable phenomenon and is an index of social morality of the country. In India the librarians are often held responsible for loss of books and have to face a difficult time in getting the loss of the books written off ... Happily the Punjab and Haryaha agricultural universities have been considerate to their librarians and have incorporated in their Accounts Code the following rule: the stock taking of the library shall ba done. once in every two years as approved by the Library Advisory Committee. The list of the books not accounted for shall be prepared and they shall be considered missing if they are not traced out by the next stocktaking.*

## CAUSES OF LOSS OF BOOKS IN LIBRARIES

Reasons for loss of books are varied. Such *loss is caused by. environmental conditions, insects and man*. Man is instrumental in the loss of books thanks *to bad habits in the handling/use of books, mutilation, pilferage of documents to meet specific needs or due to psychological reasons*. This report is limited generally to pilferage of books.

Loss due to removal of documents, depends principally on *nature of clientele, staff pattern, quality of staff, social atmosphere physical facilities and other such factors in a library.*

### (a) Physical facilities

Library, generally is accorded, a secondary position in the order of priorities. For instance, accommodation earmarked for a library is normally one of convenience to the administration rather than one in accordance with standards for library buildings. Let alone standards for library buildings, it is estimated that 90 *percent* of public libraries are housed in small buildings or part of a building having not more than 3-4 rooms. A good number of them are rented buildings. A study on college libraries reports that *"during the course of present study in which 100 college libraries were visited and 657 collage libraries were surveyed, it was revealed that none of these college libraries have their buildings strictly in accordance with the Indian standards for library building"*. It is also reported that 37.3 *percent* of schools in India do not have even a room for a library and where they have, they are used more as a storeroom. This situation stands as an impediment to equipping library buildings with adequate safeguards and introducing preventive library rules to discourage miscreants.

Besides *unplanned buildings, absence of wicket gates, property counter, inadequate lighting system and frequent power failures*, are cited as handicaps.

**(b) Personnel**

Another perennial problem is the inadequacy of staff in terms of actual workload. It is reported that management usually tend to ignore proposals on such matters. Libraries continue to function, inspite of growth at later stages, with the inadequate and/or ill-equipped staff allocated in the beginning.

**(c) Social responsibility**

The Ranganathan Committee noted that, *there are a few cirminals in the community who could neither be detected nor prevented from doing mischief*. This phenomenon prevails in all categories of libraries including academic and public libraries. It is quite a difficult task on the part of the staff to catch hold of the miscreants red-handed and prove the allegations and get through the procedure of punishment. At times enthusiastic staff may find himself isolated for this good deed.

It is believed that 90 percent of users of public libraries are students who take pride in playing mischief in the library.. Then there are the anti socials and the psychologically disturbed. However, it is also reported that the enlightened citizens also indulge in the undesirable practice of removal of books from libraries. Well-planned pilferage of valuable manuscripts and rare books is also not an uncommon matter in India. Removing of books by library staff is not rare. Added to these is the lethargy and negligance of gatekeepers. Though it is well known that documents are passed through the checking spot during peak hours or in artificial rush, not any special arrangement/caution is seen to be taken to thwart such practices. It is, however, true that physical checking may not be permissible or be resisted. It is also a known fact that more books are removed from the libraries during winter season hidden inside the heavy warmdresses or shawls, which requires special attention from the attendants. Experienced people reported that tearing of pages of documents is done in closets and such convenient places, and a shrewd attendant should be able to detect such movements.

V.I.Ps who visit libraries or borrow books are found to be another source of loss of books. Librarians find it quite hard to retrieve the books as they are not easily approachable, or the books are misplaced by them or the V.I.Ps concerned transferred to some other place.

There are also instances of books not returned to library by the staff due to transfer, death, retirement, etc. Users also fail to return borrowed books due to death, change of residence etc.

### (d) Changed Concept of Library Service

The emphasis is placed, today, on use of books than on their preservation. The underlying principle is to make maximum use of library materials by making them accessible as freely as possible to all. So libraries are liable to provide utmost access to their collections and keep them open during convenient hours of *the users*.

The open access system, though the ideal one, leads to increased loss of books due to lack of discipline and book consciousness among the users. Provision of photocopying facility is proved to be one way to reduce this menace drastically . However, the National Medical Library, New Delhi observes that inspite of photocopying facilities, mutation, tearing of pages etc. are common. The Library, therefore, is in the process of reducing photocopying charges form Re.1 to Re. 0.50 per page.

**(e) Other reasons**

(i) High cost of books :

(ii) limited supply and non-availablity of books in open market;

(iii) non-availability of multiple copies for students' use;

(iv) non-availability of adequate photocopying facilities and inter-library loan;

(v) inadequate weightage given to readers' suggestions in collection development;

(vi) urgent need for information and lack of its easy availability;

(vii) location factor of library in relation to the habitat of the users in respect of distance and inadequate transport facilities;

(viii) lack of knowledge of colletion or awareness of facilities in a library;

(ix) lack of good public relation maintained by staff; and

(x) loss during shifting of books due to flood and other reasons;

## PREVAILING SECURITY ARRANGEMENTS IN INDIA

The most common place security arrangement is one which would disallow a user to carry his/her personal effects into a library. They are supposed to be deposited at the 'materials counter'.Small bags and files may be allowed in, but files should not contain any printed material. Larger libraries have provision for wicket gate and separate doors for exit and entrance. Besides proper guarding of entrance and exit, the ventilations[9] windows etc. are covered with wire gauze so that books are not passed out of the premises. Books issued are to be carried right away out of the library which are counter checked by the security personnel at the gate as to the validity of the issue. Security is entitled to check bags and files and also challenge users in case of doubt. Users are expected to notify pre-existing damages/missing parts of a book issued before leaving the library which will be noted in the issue register or will be acknowledged by signing on the appropriate page. Documents will be checked on their return also.

It is also a practice in some libraries to supply books for use in the premises against signature and be checked when returned as a means to minimise damages to documents.

Readers are to replace damaged or lost documents or pay the value, either actual or in multiples or as assessed by the competent authority. Some libraries expect a reader to replace a whole set in case of damage to/loss of any of its volume. Some libraries like the United States Information Service, Kolkata, report that they waive payment'.for loss of books in certain special cases . Provisions for deposit of cash as a precaution against loss or damages to books is also in vogue. However, this amount as a rule is kept low for fear of its negative effect. The Guidelines for Public Library System and Services issued by the RRRLF recommends that all users should carry identity cards which would be helpful in enforcing discipline among the users especially among the students. It has been introduced in H.K.M. State Library, Bhubaneswar and was found to be working satisfactorily inspite of some initial expense and inconvenience to the users. The users on their part, it is reported,, take pride in showing their identity cards to others as a mark of distinction.

## VIGILANCE IN READING ROOMS

What all the libraries have emphasised in case of

damages to books or removal of books is the simple method of constant vigilance. It is done by the library staff and/or security staff in case of small-and medium-scale libraries, and with help of modern electronic gadgets likes short circuit video cameras in case of large libraries (Vide Appendix-4 for details of security arrangement in the National Library, Calcutta). A close watch on users either by full time attendants or by attendants or other staff has far reaching effects on loss of books. The buildings should be designed in such a way that one should. be able to see the book racks from all directions. Libraries should be properly illuminated and provision for emergency lights be made. It is also advocated that staff strength formula for open shelf system should have adequate provision for supervisory staff. Strict supervision of each level of administrative operations and fixing up of responsibilities on the persons concerned is of paramount importance. Staff who are assigned the duty of vigilance in the library should be able to book a few miscreants proportional to a certain percentage of total number of damages or losses reported in a year. These personnel need occassional guidance and proper orientation.

## PHOTOCOPYING FACILITIES

There are no two opinions on the positive effect of introduction of photocopying facilities in the libraries on damages or loss of documents. However, it is always argued that only large libraries can afford such a facility. Possession of photocopying machine, in fact, is not a must for supply of copies. There are libraries, thanks to their imagination and initiative, which are able to extend this service with the help of machines available in the vicinity. The process is that an attendant carries the documents to and from the photocopying shop and the indenter pays for the service at the shop.

## ORIENTATION PROGRAMMES AND PUBLIC RELATION

It is widely believed that orientation of freshers/new

members to the various services of a library would bring major gains to the library especially in the form of treating the books with love and care. Tactful handling (service with smile) also can pay high dividants. Good relations with the users will enlist their co-operation in keeping vigilance on other users and persuading them not to indulge in undesirable practices.

Exhibition of damaged books *and* other documents to expose the handiwork of the undesirable elements and to inculcate adequate measure of sensitivity in the minds of users will be an action in the right direction.

## STOCK VERIFICATION

Stock verification is *sine qua non* for assessing the loss of books and for identifying the misplaced books. Libraries of varying categories have their own system and span of stock verification as elaborated earlier. Stock verification should be an occasion to review existing safety arrangements and suggest improvements in including re-orientation and motivation of personnel engaged in this sphere. A librarian may plan and try to secure all such measures of security and safety as may necessitate as (a) provision of mesh work *on* openings, (b) checking of natural hazards, (c) engaging of extra staff for keeping strict and adequate viligance on all exit-points and in the stack areas where open access has been granted, (d) forming collections of items for restricted use and access, (e) modifying of library rules and procedures suitably to check mutilation and theft of library items etc., (f) envisaging strict disciplinary action against members of staff or users whose intentions are found to be doubtful or whose damaging acts have been confirmed and (g) establishment of 'Replacement Fund' for replacement of damaged or lost but useful documents. Book Replacement Fund is operated in two ways. In some cases a stipulated amount *per annum* is charged from the user. In the case of public library system in Chandigarh the amount of interest accruing annually on the library security deposited in the bank is utilized for this purpose which is reported to be quite adequate.

The auditor approach to books as consumable items or as items of store has been traditionally frowned upon by librarians. It is argued that the emphasis in stock verification should be placed more on to discover *which items* are missing than on *how much* is the loss calculated in rupee terms in the spirit of an amendment to the Rule 116 in Chapter 8 of the General Financial Rules which reads that *the position of library books, etc. is different from that of other stores.*

## NATURAL AND ENVIRONMENTAL FACTORS

Appropriate precautionary measures according to the size of a library is taken to prevent fire hazards. Very simple inexpensive arrangements with proper coaching of library staff can save a lot of books from fire. Flood is a constant threat to books in certain areas. The only solution is right choice of the building. Basements, in no case, are advisable for stocking of books.

Damages caused through environmental conditions like very high/low temperature, humidity and frost can be controlled through proper ventilation, provision of exhaust fans, room heaters etc. as the case may be and air-conditioners wherever warranted or is affordable.

The menace of insects and animals like rats, cockroaches, silverfish and white ants can be eliminated by periodical and steady pest control measures. Naphthalene, and baygon are popular and not expensive which can be used to minimise the damages. Larger libraries and specialized collections may require more modern and mechanised methods of treatments of books for preservation.,

## CONCLUSION

Finally, everything said and done, the fact remains that mutilation and removal of books is a human weakness which can only be minimised but not eliminated. So loss of books to some extent is inevitable and so they are accordingly written off. A latest technology called the Radio Frequency Identity Device (RFID) may be introduced in libraries to prevent further loss of books. This method is a little expensive one. The librarian or the staff, however, should not be penalised for such losses. However, losses beyond the permissible limit should be viewed seriously and remedial measures be taken based on recommendations.

## REFERENCES


1. ANAND (JK). Stock verification in college libraries; Some observations. *ILA Bulletin*. 17,1; January-March 1981.
2. GUPTA(SR). Stuck verification in libraries, 1990 Ken Publications, Delhi.
3. *ILA Bulletin*. 6,2-3, April-September. 1970.
4. INDIA, HUMAN RESOURCE DEVELOPMENT (Ministry of ...) National policy *on* library & information system. (Committee). (1986) (Chairman: D.P. Chattopadhyay.a). National policy on library and information & System: A presentation, 1986, Department of Culture, New Delhi.
5. INDIA, EDUCATION & YOUTH SERVICES (Ministry of ... ) LIBRARIES (Advisory Committee) (1985) (Chairman: K.P. Sinha). Report 1959. Ministry of ... New Delhi.
6. INDIA, FINANCE (Ministry of ...) Office Memorandum, dated 7 February 1984.
7. INDIA, LOK SABHA, THIRD ESTIMATES (Committee) (1965-66). Hundred and first report: Ministry of Education, Aligarh Muslim University, April 1966. Lok Sabha Secretariat, New Delhi.
8. KALIA (DR) *etal.* Guidelines for public library systems and services, Granthana : Indian Journal Library Studies. 2, 1 ; July 1991.
9. 9. NANDA (UB) GOYAL (SP). Agricultural librarianship in India; Change and continuity in fifty years of librarianship in India. Past, present and future: Seminar papers 1983. Indian Library Association, Delhi.

10. SITAL(R) CHHOTEY LAL. De-accessioning for better management of libraries. ILA Bulletin. 26,4. Jan-March 1991.

11. RANGANATHAN (SR). Library manual. For Library authorities, librarians and honorary library workers. Ed 2. 1960; Report 1962. Asia, London.

12. SAXENA (RS). Stock taking of library books and losses of books: ILA Bulletin. 17,1: January-March 1981.

13. UNIVERSITY GRANTS COMMISSION, LIBRARY (Committee). (1959) (Chairman: S.R. Ranganathan). Report: University and college libraries. 1965- University Grants Commission, New Delhi.

14. UNIVERSITY GRANTS COMMISSION, PROCEDURE ETC. OF STOCK VERIFICATION IN LIBRARIES OF CENTRAL UNIVERSITIES (Committee on) (1968) (Chairman;P.N. Wahi). Report.

## APPENDIX 1

### Existing Norms for Loss of Books in Libraries

| *S.No.* | *Agent* | *Year* | *Permissible Limit* |
|---|---|---|---|
| 1. | Ranganathan Committee of | 1959 | 2 vols. per thousand vols. issued in an open access library. |
| 2. | S.R. Ranganathan | 1960 | 3 vols. per thousand vols. issued in an open access library. |
| 3. | UGC Committee on Procedure etc. of Stock Verification in Libraries of Central Universities. | 1960 | Committee did not conclude its decision. One member suggested 5 vols.per thousand vols.issued/ consulted in a library. |
| 4. | Indian Library Association | 1969 | 4 vols. per thousand vols. issued in a library. |
| 5. | Rajasthan College Principals Conference, 1969, Bhilwara. | 1969 | 6 vols. per thousand vols. issued in a library. |
| 6. | Dhanpat Rai & Mehta. | 1970 | 0.1% to 0.33% of total stock of a library in one year. |
| 7. | Gujarat Granthalayas Sewa Sangha. | 1975 | 7 vols. per thousand vols. issued in a library. |
| 8. | R.S. Saxena. | 1981 | 2 to 4 vols. per thousand vols. circulated in a library. |
| 9. | J.K. Anand. | 1981 | 5 vols. per thousand vols. issued/ consulted in a library. |
| 10. | Ministry of Finance Government of India. | 1984 | 3 vols. per thousand vols. circulated/ consulted in a library. |

(***Source :*** Gupta (SR). Stock verification in libraries, 1990. Ken Publication, Delhi).

## APPENDIX 2

### Government of India Directives on Loss of Books

Page 40-41. Rule 116

For the existing Government of India's decision (1) below rule 116, the following shall be substituted?

"Government of India's decision (1);- The position of library books, etc. is different "from that of other stores". Accordingly, the following procedures shall be observed for purchase, write off, disposal of mutilated/damaged books and physical verification of books' in the libraries attached to the various Departments/Offices;-

(i) Librarian (Not below the rank of Deputy.,Secretary to the Govt. of India) subject to the powers delegated under Delegation of the Financial Powers rules, 1978 may purchase books etc. from the reputed and standard book-sellers on the prevalent terms and conditions. Tenders need not be called for this purpose.

(ii) *Loss of three volumes per one thousand volumes issued/consulted in a year may be taken* as reasonable provided such loss cannot be attributed to dishonesty or negligence on the part of the Librarian,, Loss of book of the *value exceeding Rs. 200/-* (Rupees two hundred) and the books of special nature and rarity shall invariably be investigated and consequential action taken. All such losses will however be writtenoff only by the competent authority.

(*iii*) Librarian who is of the rank not below Deputy Secretary to the Government of India or Head of the Department may write off the loss of volumes, mentioned in the proceeding paragraph provided the *total value of all such books, etc. does not exceed the monetary limit prescribed in the Delegation of Financial Powers Rules, 1978 for Head of a Department in respect of deficiencies and depreciations (motor cycle) included in the stock and other accounts*. In the event of the total value exceeding the monetary limit specified above, the loss of books shall be written off by the competent authority as specified in the Delegation of Financial Powers Rules, 1978.

(iv) There may be no objection to the Librarian disposing of mutilated/damaged/obsolete volumes to the best interest of the Library. However, the disposal of such volumes should be made on the recommendations of a *three member committee* to be appointed by the Administrative Ministry/Department which shall decide whether the books mutilated/damaged/obsolete are not fit for further use.

(v) Complete annual physical verification of books should be done every year in case of Libraries having not more than 20,000 volumes and not fewer than two library qualified staff. In case there is only one qualified staff the verification may be done as per sub-para. (VI)

(vi) Complete, physical verification at intervals of not more than three years should be done in the case of libraries having more than 20,000 but not more than 50,000 volumes.

(vii) Some physical verification at intervals of not more than five years may be done in the case of libraries having more than 50,000 volumes. If such a, sample verification reveals unusual or unreasonable shortages, complete verification should be done.

(viii) The verification should always be subject to surprise test check by some independent officers. The decision regarding the selection of the staff to whom this work may be entrusted, should be taken by the Administrative Ministries/Departments and Head of Department."

(Ministry of Finince O.M.No. 23(7) - E. II (A)/83 dated 7.2,1984 and C.A.G.'s U.O. No. 1964-TA.II/21-83 dated 23.12.83).

## APPENDIX 3

### Recovery of Cost of Lost Books

The Tamil Nadu Government vide G.O.MS No 1908 Education dated 11.12.84 orders recovery of cost of lost books on a percentage basis in relation to their (books) usage and age in respect of libraries under Local Library Authorities based on recommendation of Official Level Committee on Libraries (1978) which made the following observation "Loss of books in any public library is a common feature. In a way, this practice has contributed to the books being kept under lock and key by librarians in branch libraries, even though librarians are supposed to adopt open access system. The result is the reading public are either not aware of availablity of certain books or they could not take it and read when they visit the libraries. The Committee has, therefore, felt that if no recovery is made in respect of loss of books, the loss will be huge and the Local Library Authorities could not afford it".

The cost of lost books recovered from the staff is in the following order;

| | |
|---|---|
| Books more than 5 years old but less than 7 years old | 66% of the cost |
| Books over 7 years old but less than 10 years old | 50% of the cost |
| Books over 10 years old | 25% of the cost |

## APPENDIX 4

### Security Arrangement in the National Library, Kolkata

A 3-tier security system is being followed in the National Library. According to this, check posts are being maintained in all the three library buildings to see that no reading materials go outside the library. These check posts are under the Administrative Division.

The Assistant Librarians of the Reading Rooms maintain vigilance in the Reading Rooms with the help of their staff. They keep constant vigil upon the readers who come to the Library to consult the reading materials in the library.

In addition to the above, there is an independent Security Division in the Library. They scan the users during library hours from the control room with the help of four short circuit video cameras fixed in the main library building. The staff deployed in this division ensure safety and security of the Library's property against theft, pilferage and sabotage round the clock. If anyone is found involved in any short of malpractice he/she is handed over to the police for legal action. The Security Division of the libraries is detailed :

1. to keep vigilance at main building, catalogue hall and new book display hall;
2. to see that only those readers are allowed inside the building who have got valid membership cards and visitor's pass;
3. to check that no personal books/printed materials are taken inside the Library:
4. to check gate pass and movement registers etc;
5. to check bags/belongings of everybody, while going out;
6. to check the removal of waste paper and similar other materials of the Library;
7. to collect the pass and check it with the call number of

the book and make an entry in the register maintained for the purpose;

8. to see that books are going straight to the check post after issuing from the Lending Section;
9. to see that no book is going from the reading room to the general bathroom; and
10. to issue token against and articles deposited in the counter and return the articles on receipt of the particular taken.

# 14

# Library Profession and Ethics

## INTRODUCTION

*Homo sapiens* through many biogenetic revolutions developed the capacity to think and reflect. Rene Descartes, the French philosopher, aptly described it in the phrase '*cogito ergo sum*' (I think, therefore, I am) Thus human beings began to develop languages, scripts and created records. Along with history and civilization, they gathered a stockfile of data, information, knowledge and wisdom. This is categorized for convenience into disciplines or subjects.

The Greek philosophical tradition classified the knowledge into seven liberal arts for purpose of learning and education. They were called the *trivium* and *quadrivium*.

The above taxonomy of subjects was in vogue throughout the west till the end of the middle Ages. Whereas, according to the Indian philosophical tradition knowledge was grouped into *Chatushashti Kalalu* (64 arts). In modern age new subjects began to form as expounded by Ranganathan on the basis of factors like dissection, lamination, denudation, loose assemblage and superimposition. Subject formation is a continuous process, which never ends. Professions,

Occupations and Vocations develop based on growth of subjects or disciplines. Professions are not mere Occupations or Vocations, They are different in nature and character.

## WHAT IS A PROFESSION

There are various orientations towards the concept of a profession. The term profession is used to denote the whole body of persons engaged in an occupation as well as the occupation itself. An occupation attains the status of a profession by qualifying itself with an extensive education and training in a branch of science or the liberal arts. The persons involved in a profession are actually conscious of the historical and the social environment of their intellectual commitment to a subject. They act as authorities in their particualr field of vocation with an ultimate object of rendering service to the society.

### Definitions of the term Profession

*The Oxford English Dictionaty* (OED) defined the term profession as " a vocation in which a professed knowledge of some department of learning or science is used in its application to the affairs of others, in the practice of an art bounded upon it".

*The Dictionary of Social Sciences* states that "the term profession denoted occupation which demands highly specialised knowledge and skill required at least in part by courses of more or less theoretical nature and not by practice alone, tested by some form of examination either at a university or some other institution and convening to the persons, who possess their considerable authority in relation to clients".

B.M. Headicar in his book, *A Manual of Library Organisation* explains the term profession as that " it is not merely a collection of individuals who get a living for themselves by the same kind of work, nor a group organised wholly for the economic protection of its members, although, naturally this aspect is not overlooked. It is really a body of people who carry on their duties in accordance with rules designed to enforce certain standards, with two main objectives — the better protection of its members and the better service to the public".

*A Professional* : It is inferred from the above definitions that a professional is a person who practices a profession for the purpose of livelihood, gain and sometimes without charging any fee. In this mode, agriculture is the oldest profession in the world. There are other professionals like teachers, musicians, lawyers, doctors etc.

*Professionalism* : This is the art and science of practicing a profession. It involves the character, behavior, methods, ethical values, standard practices, expertise and commitment in rendering service to the public.

## Profession Vs. Vocation

The terms Vocation, Occupation, Employment, Business and Trade are. used sometimes synonymously with the term profession. But the profession has many attributes which are different from them in many respects. A profession is a service performed for the benefit of humanity and with a high sense of purpose and dedication, the main attributes of a profession in general:

- involves knowledge based intellectual activity,
- has philosophy fundamental and specific to it,
- has some specialised techniques, methods, practices and skills,
- needs an intensive education and training,
- has a set of principles, a social code and ethics of conduct and behaviour,
- has a social recognition, significance and status to its members,
- has an organisations that will find its members,
- sets specific standards for entry in training,

- has some norms and standards for the social conduct of its members,
- imposes duties and responsibilities alongwith rights, and
- is practiced as a regular occupation and leads to a service above personal gain or profit.

### Vocation and Occupation

Vocation and Occupation are terms which indicate that persons involve in them are engaged in activities for their living and personal gain. Trade, business etc are some such occupations which don't require any intensive course of education and training. An occupation or vocation involves:

- an activiy of some routine type which does not need any systematic body of knowledge,
- craft needing some skills or no skills , and
- mainly an activity involving some service against fee and sometimes rendered free.

Some of the occupations and vocations after a long standing of practice acquire certain body of knowledge and develop into a profession. In the begining librarianship was a vocation and it has gradually grew into a profession.

## LIBRARIANSHIP AS A PROFESSION

Librarianship is a broader term, inclusive of documentation and information science. In the 1950's there was some debate and discussion as they are distinct fields. J.Farradane of Great Britain started advocating that "information work is distinct from librarianship and should in no way be confused with it". This contention was not agreed by the librarians of both the Western and Eastern countries. S.R.Ranganathan said that the difference between librarianship and information science is one of degree but not kind. Documentation and Information Science are, therefore, an extension of librarianship.

The Librarianship and Information Science are dovetailed together and later brought under a rubric term, Library and Information Science. It is a single profession but not different ones. Professions have not grown overnight. There are older professions such as agriculture, medicine, teaching, music, painting etc. They were recognized and respected by society. Whereas with the explosion of information, growth of knowledge, education, industry and many other factors, new professions began to emerge over the years. Library and information Science is one such profession, which grew from occupation/vocation into a profession in the 19th century.

## As an Occupation

Librarianship as an occupation is as old as the civilizations of Mespatomia and Babylonia. There were libraries and librarians at Alexandria, Taxila, Borisippa, Nalanda as well as in the Roman Empire. Service was the motto of the libraries from the begining. Libraries were established in the ancient and medieval times by the emperors, kings, nobles and monasteries. Poets, scholars and educated elite were in-charge of libraries. Librarianship, thus, started as an occupation and employment for livelihood.

## As a Vocation

Later in the medieval ages scholars drifted away from the librarianship. With the establishment of more and more libraries, development of printing and publishing of books in Europe, a special class of educated people began to assume the role of librarianship. They were not trained and there were no special courses in librarianship. During these initial stages librarians began to develop certain skills and methods by trial and error. Their practices were rudimentary. This was the stage when the librarianship was only an vocation but not a profession. There was no code of ethics and professional brotherhood except the purpose of service to the public.

## As a Profession

With the industrialization in the European countries, information and knowledge began to grow geometrically. New type of institutions of learning like mechanics, Polytechnics, research institutions, universities and scholarly organizations came into existence. All these institutions needed well-organized libraries. The establishment of the British Museum(London), Bibliotheca Nationale (Paris) and the Library of Congress (Washington, D.C) was the turning point. The development of various types of libraries and the enactment of the first library legislation by the British Parliament in 1850 provided the sound footing to the profession. Publication of seminal books such as Melwil Dewey's *Decimal Classification, Cutter's Rules for a Dictionary Catalogue,* founding of Library Association (UK), American Library Association (USA) and the starting of first library school in 1887 in the USA, ushered in the librarianship into a profession, first in the west and later in the East. During the last 150 years, the library profession fast developed into a strong and vibrant profession.

Library and Information Science with a strong social philosophy of service, is a composite discipline comprehending within itself a variety of subjects and has attained an independent status of a social science. LIS possesses the required attributes to call it a profession.

- It has a body of specialized knowledge and terminology for the purpose of teaching in library schools.
- It has a set of principles, norms, laws, professional code and values.
- LIS has a large number of Organizations/Associations for different groups at different levels in all the countries of the world.
- It is committed to an ideal of free and fair service to society.

- It is committed to maintain standards and quality in the work of the practitioners of the profession.
- It has social recognition, providing social status to its practitioners, protection, power and privileges. This raises the LIS profession to the dignity of a learned profession.

## KNOWLEDGE BASE OF LIS PROFESSION

Knowledge is the *summum bonnum* of any profession. Librarianship *for a long time was based* on adhoc rules and practices. These were later improved and refined on trial and error basis. Professionals based on their experience began to publish manuals, rules and guides on several library activities for the benefit of other professionals. The profession during its existence of one hundred and fifty years developed scientific principles, normative principles, canons, laws, postulates etc. Establishment of library schools and associations provided opportunity to the professionals to discuss, debate and research on the fundamental issues concerned the LIS profession. Special terminology also came into vogue. S.R.Ranganathan himself contributed more than 600 specialized terminology.

Professionals started publishing theoretical literature in the field. Classification schemes such as DDC, LC, CC, UDC, Cataloguing rules like the Brilish Museum Cataloguing Rules, Rules for a Dictionary Catalog, AACR, CCC, CCF, ISBD, ISBN, ISSN etc. have laid the strong foundation to the LIS profession. S.R.Ranganathan through his books, *Five Laws of Library Science* and *Prolegomena* strengthened the knowledge base of LIS profession beyond question. These and many other developments laid foundations to various branches of LIS and made it a full-fledged science. The knowledge base of LIS profession is constantly replenished with new concepts and principles from the data derived from research in the LIS schools. Developments in computer science, Information Technology, Communication Technology, multimedia and networking widened the knowledge base of the LIS.

In the day to day administration of library, practical skills are needed in the profession. These involve the ability to handle the hardware, software and humanware. User education, User studies, resource management and sharing added to the core of theoretical and practical knowledge of the profession. Multidisciplinary mix of the LIS profession is the strength of the profession.

## EDUCATION AND TRAINING FOR THE LIS PROFESSIONALS

Intensive education and specialized training are yet other attributes of a profession. For discharging their duties with efficiency and to interact with the users of library effectively, the LIS professionals should possess the necessary qualifications, experience, training, innovative capability, proper attitude and aptitude and dedicated spirit towards the professional work. In the initial stages of the profession, there were two modes of training in existence. The British model had a tradition of strong professional body like the LA, directly responsible for providing professional qualifications. Whereas the continental and American model believed in imparting professional education through academic institutions like colleges and universities. Presently there is only one model of professional education i.e the university based professional education. The period of professional education is long. Professional education is however a life long process in view of the continuous generation of new knowledge, methods, practices and skills.

### LIS Schools

Library schools are important as they impart the necessary education and training to the would be professionals. Melvil Dewey started the first library school in 1887. With the growth and development of public, academic and special libraries in 20th century in all countries, more library schools were opened in universities. In schools and polytechnics in some countries LIS is taught as optional subject. At the university level BLISc, MLISc and integrated MLISc courses are conducted. Besides the regular Distance Education academic courses, the Department so LIS provides also in-service courses, refresher courses and orientation courses.

LIS schools are proliferating very fast in India. Before 1947 there were only two library schools. At present according to the CDC report (2001) there are 75 library schools. Library Associations and Institutions conduct certificate courses in all the states in India.

### LIS Teachers

Teaching should be absolutely free from any bias whatsoever. This is necessary as students are largely influenced by their teachers. Therefore, it is imperative that the LIS teacher should present a complete and integrated picture of the subject.

Teachers determine what knowledge, skills and attitudes are needed for the library activities at present and in future. In some cases teaching is made as the faculty members learnt during their times. With the result, the students receive somewhat out-of-date education, which makes them obsolete. The teachers have a crucial role in preparing and motivating the students in the subject as well as in the profession. Teachers are the trendsetters. They have to train the students to become high-class information managers who can effectively serve their users.

### LIS Syllabi

The LIS schools have to revise, modify and expand their curriculum from time to time. Old and obsolete portions of the syllabi are to be replaced with new concepts and developments in the professional knowledge base and practical skills. Application of computers, communication and multimedia technologies have opened up new vistas in the LIS. So the course curriculum should be changed to include these items to prepare the LIS students to the new environment.

### Apprenticeship

The new entrants into the LIS get their theoretical knowledge through their education in LIS schools. Theoretical education alone is not sufficient to the new professionals. They should learn many intricacies and handsome experience in practical management of a library. Management skills, technological skills, communication skills, statistical skills etc. are to be learnt through "the apprenticeship. Sometimes it is said that the real education starts after leaving the university."

### Attitude and Apitude

LIS work is not an occupation or vocation for livelihood. It is a noble service committed to the public. The entrants should have proper understanding of the social philosophy of the profession. They should have basic aptitude and feel responsibility of duty to readers, documents and staff. The attitude of the mind is most important than any amount of training.

## PROFESSIONAL ETHICS

Ethics is yet an another essential element of the LIS profession. Ethics is science of morals. A set of moral principles are necessary for any professional group including the LIS professionals in order to regulate and guide their conduct and behavior in their day to day activities.

The term ethics is derived from the Greek word '*ethos*' which means good conduct. Ethics is a branch of philosophy, which is concerned with human character and conduct. Every profession with no exception of LIS seeks justification of its occupation in terms of a set of moral principles or values. Agnes F.P.Greer in his article, *Professional ethics for Library workers*, says that ethics "is science of right conduct and character; the science which treats of the nature and grounds of moral obligation; the doctrine of man's duty in respect of himself and the rights of others. These rules applied to one's profession, then constitute professional ethics". The concept of professional ethics signifies the system or code of morals of a particular profession.

## Ethics for LIS Professionals

LIS is a noble and learned profession. Its motto is service to mankind. The idea of ethics came to the forefront in the profession in 1876 with the establishment of the American Library Association. The word 'ethics' was used for the first time at the ALA conference at Boston in 1908. The ALA appointed a number of committees after 1922 to draft a code of ethics.

## ALA Code of Ethics

The American Library Association (ALA) after prolonged debates and discussions adopted a professional code of ethics in 1938, which was later revised in 1975 and 1981. The ALA code stated the norms and regulations for librarians in relation to (a) the governing authority (b) their constituency (c) fellow employees with in the library (d) profession and (e) society. The American Association for Information Science (AS1S) also brought out a draft code of ethics in 1990.

## LA Code of Ethics

The Library Association (UK) appointed a working party on professional ethics in 1978 to draft an ethical code. The draft code, thus prepared by the working party was adopted by the Library Association (LA) in 1983. The features of the code relate to (a) the competence of the librarian (b) the question of discretion and respect to a client's privacy (c) professional independence and intellectual freedom (d) the impartiality of library profession (e) financial ethics, and (f) the integrity of members.

## Indian Attempts

Indian Library and Information Science professionals also are keenly interested in evolving an ethical code to the profession-. These efforts remained for long at the level of survey of literature on professional ethics. A.K.Mukherjee,

R.L.Mittal, Meganand and Amitabh Chaterjee highlighed the topic in their books and articles. These are all feeble attempts.The only effort to consider this subject seriously in a professional forum was at the IASLIC conference in 1984. It raised discussion and resulted in a resolution for a professional ethical code. Later in 1986 The Joint Council of Library Associations in India (JCOLAI) discussed the issue and made a set of recommendations. Thus the professional ethical code in India remained at drafting level.

## Facet of Ethics For Inclusion in the Code

LIS professionals in course of their work interact with different user groups besides the documents and their own staff. Professionals have duty and responsibility to all of them. They need competence to perform their work. There are many problems, which the ethical code should cover. Problems such as:

- Librarian and the library authority
- Librarian and the staff
- Librarian and the readers
- Librarian and the book trade
- Librarian and the documents
- Librarian himself
- Librarian and the profession
- Librarian and the associations
- Librarian and the society
- Librarian and laws of the land.

The ethical principles should remind the professionals time and again his role, duties, responsibilities and commitment to the public service. A personal oath on the model of doctors oath at the time of entry into the profession is necessary to the LIS professionals also.

Professional associations is another attribute of a

profession. Members of a profession advocating paternity to each other come together and form an association or organization for some common purpose.' The earliest library association is the ALA, which was formed in 1876. Later the LA (1877), ASLIB (1926), IFLA (1929), FID, ILA, IASLIC and many more such LIS professional associations and Organisations were founded in all the countries of the world. The associations strive hard to focus on professional problems and set up high standards in service. They have the following tasks before them.

- To create awareness among the professionals for a common cause,
- To foster a sense of unity, equality and fellowship among the various levels of professionals,
- To influence and guide the authorities in creating and maintaining high standards of training,
- To exchange ideas and discuss technical problems for improving the management and working of libraries,
- To establish standards and a code for professional work,
- To organize systematically continuing education programs in order to keep the professionals abreast with the latest developments in the field,
- To establish and maintain laisen with government and sister associations and organisations,
- To fight for the common goal and protect the professional interests,
- To encourage, create and motivate professionalism and leadership,
- To protect the members of the profession from harassment of the authorities.

The professional associations should not work at cross-purpose. There should be consideration and cooperation amongst them, otherwise the rivalries will weaken them.

The L1S is an interdisciplinary subject with a blend of philosophies, theories and practices from different sources. Information is recognized as an important resource. Its contribution for the economic and cultural growth of society is beyond question. The LIS profession is engaged in generation, collection, classification, storage, retrieval, manipulation, management repacking, evaluation, dissemination and marketing of information. Its role in the well being of the society is well recognized.

### Social Significance

LIS profession is a noble profession with an ideal of service to others. It includes duties and responsibilities commensurating with rights and privileges. LIS professionals are party to social contact with ethical overtones. The profession as a while has been striving hard to maintain standards, preventing abuse of position and serving the society to the best of its ability.

### Recognition

A profession comes into existence only when society recognizes its value and services. On the basis of importance of the profession, society provides to it power, privileges and status. The LIS profession is recognized through out the world as a learned profession. Its role in Information and Knowledge societies is crucial and central. The social status of the LIS professionals in developed countries well recognized.

## LIS PROFESSION IN INDIA

Libraries were there in India from the ancient times. But public libraries began to be established only during the British rule. The Calcutta public library (1835), the Cannemara Public Library (1890) and the Imperial Library (1902) were established. Many public libraries in smaller towns and villages were started. With the founding of universities and colleges after the Wood's, Despatch (1857) the academic libraries began to grow. During the national movement in the first half of the twentieth century public libraries began to inspire the minds of men.

LIS education started in India in 1911 with the establishment of a library school at Baroda by William Alanson Boden who was invited by the Maharaja Sayaji Rao Gaykwad of Baroda for establishing libraries in his state. Asa Don Dickenson started the second library school in 1915 at Lahore University in undivided India. Andhra Desa Grandhalaya Bandagara Sangham was founded in 1914 and this institution started conducting library classes from 1919. The turning point in library education was he starting of library course in Madras University by S.R.Ranganathan in 1929. S.R.Ranganthan with his multifaceted role as librarian, teacher, writer and research guide laid a strong foundation to the library profession in India. Today the LIS courses are taught at 85 universities at different levels from Diploma to Ph.D.

The first book on librarianship was published in 1912 under the title, *Hints on Library Administration* by B.H.Mehta. Ranganathan's contribution to library literature was enormous. His works, *Five Laws of Library Science, Prolegomena to Library Classification, Colon Classification, Classified Catalogue Code, Library Administration* etc have become would famous and added to the knowledge base of the LIS profession. Library literature even today in India is an ever-increasing phenomena.

The first library journal *The Library Miscellany* was started in 1912. *Grandhalaya Sarvaswam* in Telugu was started in 1915. There are today 50 journals in LIS in India both in English and Indian languages. There are several forums for library professionals to express their ideas and experiences.

The first library Association, the Andhra Desa Grandhalaya Bandagara Sangham which in later years renamed as Andhra Pradesh Library Association was started in 1914 by Ayyanki Venkataramanaiah and others at Vijayawada. There after other associations such as Punjab

Library Association (1916), Bengal Library Association (1925), Madras Library Association (1928), Indian Library Association (1933) and Indian Association of Special Libraries and Information Centres (1955) were formed. There are today more than one-library associations in every state in India. At the National level new bodies such as the AGLIS, SIS, CALIBER, NACLIS etc. have appeared. These associations conduct their annual seminars, conferences, and conventions providing the library professionals opportunities to express their thoughts, views and ideas.

The first library legislation was enacted in the Madras State in 1948. Today 17 states out of 29 states have enacted library legislation. Library legislation is on the anvil in more states in the years to come.

The library profession with variety of libraries like public, academic and special libraries has a wide scope to expand and develop in India. Though the profession is increasing day by day, quality of education and services have not commensurately increased. Library schools have to reform their syllabi including provision for Information technology. They should be provided with proper classrooms and computer laboratories. Research facilities in LIS are to be strengthened.

## CONCLUSION

Homo Sapiens through their capacity to think and reflect create a stockfile of information resulting in knowledge and wisdom. With the exposition of information and knowledge base new disciplines are being created through the. different process of dissection, lamination etc as stated by S.R.Ranganathan. The disciplines when practiced by people for the good of others in society attained the attributes such as formation of knowledge base by criteria of justification and variety, extensive education and training in the specific field, formation of an ethical code of conduct etc. There are many professions such as agriculture, medicine; law, music, painting etc. Professions are not static, and grow with the needs and requirements of the society.

The LIS is one such profession and libraries are there from ancient times. Poets, scholars and educated elite maintained them. There were no scientific principles for the organization of documents. As the libraries began to grow due to industrial revolution and advent of printing a special class of people emerged to manage libraries. The publication of theoretical works like Dewey Decimal Classification, Rules for Dictionary Catalogue, Five Laws of Library Science, CCC, AACR, Prolegomena to Library Science turned the librarianship into a profession with a strong knowledge base. Special and intensive library education and training started with the founding of the first library school in USA in 1887 and many educational institutions today all over the world are imparting education in LIS varying from certificate course to Ph.D. degree. In India LIS education started by W.A.Borden and Asa Don Dickenson and at present 85 universities are offering LIS courses.

A profession needs an ethical code to regulate the conduct and behavior of its members. LIS profession in order to systematize, the relations of its members with the library authorities, books, book trade, co-workers and reader groups needed an ethical code. The ALA and LA have formulated ethical codes in 1935 and 1980, which were later revised and reformulated. In India JOCLAI in 1986 made certain recommendations towards formulation of the ethical code, but yet to come out.

There are many LIS professional associations throughout the world such as ALA, LA, ASLIB, FID, IFLA, ILA, IASLIC etc. to create awareness, protect from authorities and to establish standards. India had libraries in ancient and medieval times. At present there are 68,000 public libraries, 300 university libraries, about 80,00 college libraries and many special libraries.

Library Journals and library literature are on increase. S.R.Ranganathan had set the tone and wave to the LIS profession in India. The profession has to keep up the quality and standards now and as well as in the future. The image and impact of libraries is growing is growing gradually as a crucial sector for national develoment.

## REFERENCES

1. Bhattacharya,G. "Library Profession, . Library Science and Ranganathan". *In Venkatappaiah, V(Gen. ed) March of Librarianship. Kaula Festschrift.* Bombay: Vikas Publishing House, 1979. p.42-48.
2. Bhattacharya, G and Mukherjee, B.P. "Professional ethics for information service". *In Prabin Roy Choudhary and Mukhopadhyay, N (Eds). Library and Information Services in India. Dr.S.M. Ganguly commemorative volume.* Calcutta: IASLIC, 2000. pp. 107-121.
3. Binwal, J.C. " Characteristics of the library profession and its status in India and Meghalaya". *In Mahapatra, P.K. and Thomas, V.K (Eds). Public libraries in developing countries: status and trends.* New Delhi: Vikas Publishing House, 1996.
4. Kumar, P.S.G. *Foundations of Information Science.* New Delhi: S.Chand, 1998 (See chapter 29.p.298-305).
5. Mittal, R.L. "Ethics of Librarinaship". *In MITTAL, R.L. Library administration: theory and practice.* 4th ed. Delhi: Metropolitan, 1978 (See chapter 3).
6. Sanhi, Neera. " Profession, Professional socialization and role theory". *In Chopra, H.R. et al (Eds). Library science and its facets.* New Delhi: Ess Ess publications, 1998.
7. Thompson, James. *A history of the principles of librarianship.* London: Clive Bingley, 1977.
8. Turner, C and Hodge, M.N. " Occupation and professions". *In Jackson, J.A (Ed). Professions and professionalism.* Cambridge: Cambridge University Press, 1970. pp. 26-30.

# 15

# WHY LIBRARIES ARE STARVED OF BOOKS

Books, readers and staff are the three components of a library. H.G. Wells once said : "Books are the refuge and reservoir of power... Men may suffer and men may die, but human thought embodied in science and literature goes marching on. Let us get back to enduring things. Let us get back to our books." Books are, therefore, the vehicles of knowledge and the life-blood of education. No educational institution can be without them. Thomas Cerlyle said : "The true university of these days is a collection of books." Therefore, on the strengths and weaknesses of university libraries depend the standard and quality of university education.

The number of books published in the country every year showed an increase during the seventies and the early eighties. It should have risen further follcwing expansion of educator, but has begun to decline. The number of publications every year for the last one decade will not go beyond 17,000 titles. And most of them are either fiction or religious in character. Books of serious nature and on subjects of specialisation are few.

Indian libraries, therefore, depend more and more on imported books in science, technology, communication, the social sciences and the like. Until recently the country was spending around Rs. 60 crores annually on the import, of books. This figure is rising every year for various reasons.

In the last one decade, the prices of hardbacks have trebled and of paperbacks more than doubled. The reason is the increased cost of paper and of labour. This is affecting the library budgets of Indian universities.

This apart is the increasing exchange rates of foreign currencies, particularly the dollar and the pound, vis-a-vis the Indian rupee. The rates have gone up by 146 per cent to 340 per cent in the last 10 years. This too is cutting into the library budgets.

Consequently, the intake of books by university libraries has considerably declined. Instead of library editions, they are purchasing paper backs which cannot withstand the wear and tear of use. Because of the price boom, it has become difficult for them to purchase even paperbacks because their budgets have not increased in porportion to the rise in prices and in exchange rates.

In the last 40 years, there has been a proliferation of universities in India. Their number increased from 20 in 1947 to 360 in 2008. But the allocation for education during the seventh Five Year Plan and the subsequent years has not touched even 2 per cent of the national budget. The budgetary provision has remained static though the institutions sharing it have increased.

Various commissions and committees such as the Rgdhakrishnan Commission, the Kothari Commission and the UGC Library Committee (1957) had suggested various types of allocation to the university libraries. But no definite pattern of allocation is yet discernible. There are wide variations in what was recommended and what was provided.

An analysis of the budgetary provisions of 99universities based on the data given in the "Universities Handbook 1985-

86" showed that the percentage of library allocation to the total university budget ranged from a meagre 0-1 in the case of 23 libraries to a little over 10 per cent in respect of just 11 libraries. The average was 3-4 per cent. This indicates the poor finance that the university libraries are provided with to equip themselves with books and periodicals to make their collections useful for both teaching and research.

To ease this situation, the Association of Indian Universities (AIU) has suggested that upto 10 per cent of the university budget should be made available to the libraries. Dr. K. N. Raj, in his report on Karnataka universities, has recommended that the libraries should get at least 20 per cent of the university budget.

From all these, two points stand out — that the budgetary provision for books and periodicals should be increased from time to time, and the library budgets should be linked to the university's total budget. With an increase in the university's total budget the budgetary provision for the libraries should automatically rise thus offsetting the rise in prices of publications and in the exchange rates. The provision for libraries should be at least 20 per cent of the total university budget

Other points worth considering are:

— University libraries should share resources and avoid purchasing outdated foreign titles.

— A comprehensive network of such libraries should be established for effective resource sharing and inter-library lending.

— They, should build up specialised collections in co-operation with other libraries in the area or region to avoid duplication and wastage.

— Indian publishers should develop relations with international publishers and secure the copyright for publishing important foreign books in India at a cheaper price.

— Foreign publishers should bring out cheaper editions of their books for the benefit of the Third World countries

— Indian publishers and the Government of India should take care not to import left-overs from the foreign book market and titles weeded out of foreign university libraries.

— University libraries should be provided with modern telecommunication facilities for obtaining blbliographical information.

— The publishers and the Government of India should seriously think of evolving a pricing policy for books.

# 16

# SOURCES AND SERVICES IN THE HUMANITIES : A PROPOSAL FOR NHDC

## INTRODUCTION

The 'universe of knowledge' is broadly divided into three areas namely—the Humanities, the Social Sciences and the Natural Sciences. Of these, the humanities are far older and may most appropriately be described as venerable. The humanities is the mother of all other sciences. The purpose of the humanities as described by E.H. Gombrich is that of "recovery, preserving and interpreting the cultural heritage of mankind".

## DEFINITIONS

Some of the definitions of the humanities are as follows:

**(i) Encyclopaedia Britannica (Vol. II)** : "Humanities; a group of educational disciplines distinguished in content and method from the physical and biological sciences, and if, less decisively, from the social sciences. The group includes language and literature in each of their principal examples (ancient and modern), the fine arts other than literature, philosophy, at least in its more traditional divisions, and, to a less clearly defined extent, history where the boundary between the social sciences and the humanities is most debatable. These are the core of the humanities and are sometimes organized as a school or division in the modern university. The humanities are studies which centre attention on the life of man. But, this does not by itself serve to distinguish them from biology, a natural science, if it directs its attention to man ; or from politics, a social science (for man, as Aristotle said, is a political animal) or even from religion (for man, as Edmund Burke added, is a religious animal). The Humanities stand committed to no particular philosophy or creed, they assume the possibility of distinguishing with some sharpness between man and the rest of nature and between the human and supernatural".

**(ii) The Encyclopedia Americana (Vol. 14) :** The term 'humanities' means the branches of learning that deal with human thought and culture, excluding the sciences. The term was applied originally to the study of the literatures, of classical Greece and Rome. It has since been expanded to cover all languages and literatures, the Arts, History and Philosophy. The humanities, as generally defined in the modern educational curriculum, are treated in the Encyclopedia Americana in hundreds of articles such as Architecture, Arts, Dance, Drama, History, Language, Literature, Music, Philosophy, and Theology.

**(iii) Longman Dictionary of Contemporary English (1978) :** Humanities are studies such as literature, the languages of ancient Greece and Rome, history etc., the Arts : those subjects or fields of study that are not considered to be part of science.

**(iv) Collins Cobuild English Language Dictionary (1987) :** "Humanities are the subjects of study such as literature, philosophy and history which are concerned with human beings, their ideas, actions and relationships rather than the science subjects."

However, the humanities elude precise definition. The boundaries of the humanities are fuzzy. The following subjects constitute the humanities : 1) Languages (both classical and modern); 2) Linguistics : 3) Literature ; 4) History ; 5) Jurisprudence ; 6) Philosophy ; 7) Archaeology ; 8) Arts ; 9) Folklore ; 10) Theology and Religious Studies. Those aspects of social sciences which have humanistic content and employ humanistic methods.

## INFORMATION EXPLOSION

For a long time libraries and humanistic studies were regarded synonymous. The humanities studies are based on libraries and its scholars require a large number of books. Further, the scholars insist on direct access to the books and documents in their fields. Hence, the library constitute the laboratory of the scholars in the humanities.

In the 20th century however, as the survey of Andrela reveals, the literature even in the humanities has witnessed an exponential growth doubling every 10 to 15 years. This has radically changed the position of the scholarship in humanities. Hence, there is a growing awareness that the humanistic scholarship also need the indexing and abstracting services and documentation and bibliographic control. Eugene Garfield in his preface to the *Arts and Humanities Citation Index* stated that : "1) The Arts and Humanities, no less than the sciences, need a large scale index that provides multi-disciplinary coverage ; 2) An uptodate service issued on a current basis and cumulated annually would be welcomed ; and 3) There was widespread belief in the potential effectiveness of citation and title-word indexing in Arts and Humanities information retrieval."

## HUMANISTIC SCHOLARSHIP

Humanistic scholarship is equally important as the scholarship in sciences and social sciences, for the progress and development of the human kind. In this connection

Dr. Sarvapalli Radhakrishnan in the *Report of the University Education Commission* (1948-49) said ' When the man in the street speaks of research, he generally thinks of research in natural sciences, but educated men cannot undervalue the mutual relations of the different departments of knowledge, the primary philosophical truths to which we cannot attach a materialistic value, and all that retrospective knowledge which in the largest sense is called History. If we develop a community with a large amount of material knowledge, power and energy, with more or less of an absence of widespread influences of humanities, it will be in a perilous condition in a crisis for lack of that enlarged knowledge, philosophical thinking, and refinement of sympathies and tastes which we owe to the humanities. Only by a combination of sciences and humanities can a true conception of civilisation survive".

## INDIAN SCENARIO

The tables 1, 2 and 3 reveal the present position of the research in the field of Humanities in India : The Table-1 shows faculty-wise distribution of student enrolment for the five years period 1986-87 to 1990-91. It reveals enrolment in each faculty as a percentage of total enrolment in all the faculties taken together. It will be seen that enrolment in the faculty of Arts (including Oriental Learning) has been the highest as percentage of total enrolment in each year, followed by the faculty of Commerce, Science and Law in that order. Year to year variations in the percentage of enrolment in each faculty to total enrolment in all the faculties taken together have been a very marginal nature. For example, enrolment in the faculty of Arts has been 40.4 per cent in each of the two years 1989-90 to 1990-91. Similarly, in the faculty of Commerce, the enrolment percentage was 21.3 in 1989-90 and 21.9 in 1990-91. Percentage share of the faculty of Science remained 19.6 during 1989-90 to 1990-91. Enrolment trends in other faculties present a similar picture except that percentage shares of these

**Table 1. Student Enrolement in the Universities : Faculty Wise 1986-87 to 1990-91**

| Course of Study | 1986-87 | | 1987-88 | | 1988-89 | | 1989-90 | | 1990-91 | |
|---|---|---|---|---|---|---|---|---|---|---|
| | Enrolement | % of Total | Enrolement (estimated) | % of Total | Enrolement (estimated) | % of Total | Enrolement (estimated) | % of Total | Enrolement (estimated) | % of Total |
| Arts (including oriental learning) | 14,83,794 | 40.3 | 15,37,210 | 40.3 | 15,91,012 | 40.3 | 17,17,437 | 40.4 | 17,89,480 | 40.3 |
| Science .. | 7,25,328 | 19.7 | 7,51,440 | 19.7 | 7,77,740 | 19.7 | 8,34,087 | 19.6 | 8,69,119 | 19.5 |
| Commerce .. | 7,91,602 | 21.5 | 8,20,100 | 21.5 | 8,48,804 | 21.5 | 9,31,882 | 21.3 | 9,69,882 | 21.5 |
| Education .. | 84,683 | 2.3 | 87,732 | 2.3 | 90,803 | 2.3 | 95,979 | 2.3 | 99.613 | 2.3 |
| Engineering Technology .. | 1,69,336 | 4.6 | 1,75,463 | 4.6 | 1,81,604 | 4.6 | 2,09,371 | 4.9 | 2,16,837 | 4.9 |
| Medicine .. | 1,32,547 | 3.6 | 1,37,319 | 3.6 | 1,42,125 | 3.6 | 1,42,270 | 3.4 | 1,50,458 | 3.4 |
| Agriculture .. | 47,864 | 1.3 | 49,587 | 1.3 | 51,323 | 1.3 | 46,229 | 1.1 | 46,908 | 1.1 |
| Veterinary Science | 11,046 | 0.3 | 11,443 | 0.3 | 11,844 | 0.3 | 10,957 | 0.3 | 11,063 | 0.3 |
| Law .. | 2,13,549 | 5.8 | 2,21,236 | 5.8 | 2,28,979 | 5.8 | 2,22,961 | 5.3 | 2,34,538 | 5.3 |
| Others .. | 22,091 | 0.6 | 22,887 | 0.5 | 23,628 | 0.6 | 36,822 | 0.8 | 37,349 | 0.8 |
| Total | 36,81,870 | 100.0 | 38.14,417 | 100.0 | 39,47,922 | 100.0 | 42,46,878 | 100.0 | 44,25,247 | 100.0 |

faculties in total enrolment have been far too small as compared to the faculties of Arts, Commerce and Science.

**Table 2. Number of doctoral dissertations accepted by the Indian Universities during the period 1857-1970**

| *Area* | *Number of Dissertation Accepted* | *Percentage* |
|---|---|---|
| Physical Sciences | 8062 | 39.34 |
| Biological Sciences | 4197 | 20.48 |
| Humanities | 5415 | 26.42 |
| Social Sciences | 2819 | 13.76 |
| Total | 20493 | 100 |

The above table reveals that about 60 per cent of research is done in the area of physical sciences and biological sciences, followed by the humanities (about 26 per cent) and social sciences (about 14 per cent).

Another indicator of the emphasis on the humanities research is provided by the number of major research projects approved by the University Grants Commission during the period 1974-75 to 1982-83. (Table 3).

**Table 3. Number of major research projects approved by the University Grants Commission during 1974-75 to 1982-83**

| *Area* | *Number of major Research Projects* |
|---|---|
| Humanities ... ... | 224 |
| Social Sciences ... ... | 117 |
| Professional Subjects ... | 68 |
| (e.g. Commerce, Library & Information Science, Teacher Education, Business Management, etc) | |

The University Grants Commission annual reports during the period 1974-75 to 1982-83. (Table 3)

A subject analysis of these projects shows that the

humanities subjects have the highest number of research projects when compared to social sciences and professional subjects ; the modern Indian languages top the list with 68 projects, history has 63 projects and linguistics has 14 projects. It may be mentioned here that humanities research ranks second, being next only to physical sciences and biological science in the quantum of research output.

## BIBLIOGRAPHIC CONTROL

After independence in 1947 the Government of India established for the humanities research various bodies such as Academy of Letters (Sahitya Akademi), Academy of Fine Arts (Lalit Kala Akademi) and Academy of Music, Dance and Drama (Sangeet Natak Akademi). These institutions were meant only to encourage the creative talent. They were not provided with information teeth or activities concerning documentation and bibliographic control. There is no 'National Information System' for the humanities so far. There are various organisations working in this field. There is a need to have the Humanities Information System at the national level to co-ordinate the diverse elements of Indian scenario in harmony in the area of the humanities.

In the field of Sciences and Social Sciences various Councils and Documentation Centres had come up after 1947. For Science and Technology, CSIR was established to cater to the information needs of the Scientists and Technologists. INSDOC was established in 1952. As far as the Social Sciences are concerned, there is an effective bibliographic control at the national and international levels. In the case of Social Sciences, ICSSR was established in 1972 and its documentation centre namely NASSDOC came into existence subsequently. Only the humanities are left out without any bibliographic control in this multilingual country, with diverse elements of customs, cultures and religions. Some years ago the University Grants Commission proposed to set up a National Information Centre for the Humanities in one of the Universities in India on par with the Information Centre for Science established at the Indian Institute of Science, Bangalore and Information Centres for Social Sciences established at the S.N.D.T. Women's University, Mumbai and at the M.S. University, Baroda. The Information Centre for the humanities hasn't so far come into existence.

In India, we do not have adequate bibliographic apparatus to serve the needs of the humanities scholars. The secondary services such as bibliographic, abstracting and indexing services are non-existent in most subjects and in subjects which have such services they are grossly inadequate. It is distressing to note that we are unable to bring out even the monthly issues of *Indian National Bibliography* regularly. There is an urgent need to compile retrospective bibliographies of collections scattered in various humanities libraries throughout India. We do have indexing services such as *Guide to Indian Periodical Literature* and *Index India.* But, their coverage of humanities subjects is not comprehensive. Many special libraries are bringing out .documentation lists but no effort has been made to consolidate and co-ordinate their services. It may be emphasized that for proper resource sharing we should have a comprehensive indexing service (backed up with efficient photocopy service) at the national level in each of the humanities subjects.

## CONCLUSION

Resource sharing is an omnibus term denoting many aspects such as co-operative acquisition, co-operative cataloguing and classification, co-operative storage and delivery, co-operative automation, inter-library loans, etc. It implies pooling of resources and sharing of functions and services by the participating libraries for their mutual benefit. The entire experience demonstrates over and over again that "no man is an island and neither is a library" and resource sharing is "the life style of future libraries". Any resource sharing presupposes the following four variables :

(i) Resource (collection) ; (ii) Tools to know the resource; (iii) Professional cadre with motivation to utilise the resource ; and (iv) the User.

The above four variables are essential for the 'building up of an infrastructure for any resource sharing in every subject. In India, in the case of the humanities these variables are scattered throughout the country and there is no apex body to co-ordinate the information services in humanities. Because of this the various Indian languages, literatures, arts, music, etc are at a disadvantage to assimilate the diverse regional trends into a unified personality. This is affecting to a large extent even the national integration as the regional literatures and arts are operating as centrifugal forces. In order to curb this type of regionalism in literatures and arts of this vast country of ours and to channelise the regional literatures and arts into a multidirectional native personality, a national documentation centre for the humanities is a must.

The proposed National Humanities Documentation Centre (NHDC) may be based at New Delhi with regional centres at Kolkata, Mumbai and Hyderabad to cater to the needs of eastern, western and southern regions of India respectively. We have many bodies concerned with the humanities such as public libraries, private libraries, academic libraries, special libraries, professional societies, archives, museums, etc. working in isolation. These bodies have to be structured into a network for close co-operation. This can be done through the guidance and co-ordination by the NHDC. The NHDC can perform a variety of functions such as :

(i) Compilation of union catalogues of the humanities periodicals; (ii) Preparation of current and retrospective bibliographies of the humanities collections in major libraries of India ; (iii) Preparation of retrospective cumulated indexes of the Indian humanities periodicals; (iv) Collection and preservation of manuscripts and artistic creations; (v) Acquistion of doctoral dissertations and research reports in the humanities subjects ; (vi) Maintenance of an upto date register of research in progress in the humanities; (vii) Assisting researchers through study grants for visiting libraries; (viii) Providing efficient reprography and microfilming services; (ix) Offering translation services from regional languages and foreign languages; (x) Preparation of directories of the humanities scholars such as writers, artists, etc., and also of institutions engaged in the study and research of the humanities; (xi) Providing current awareness services like documentation lists, lists of additions, SDI service, etc. (xii) Undertaking area study bibliographies to consolidate all humanities source documents worthy of research, belonging to different states and union territories irrespective of their form or language ; (xiii) Rendering bibliographic service on request : (xiv) Exploring the possibility of establishing inter-library resource centres to serve as depositories ; (xv) Acting as a clearing agency for the exchange of information on all humanities subjects ; and (xvi) Serving as the National Centre for co-operation with other national and international agencies. It is to be pointed out that all the above functions have a bearing on the document delivery system in the humanities.

## REFERENCES


1. GOMBRICH (E.A.). Research in humanities : ideals and idols. *Daedalus*. 102, 3 ; 1973 ; 1-10.
2. INDIA. UNIVERSITY EDUCATION COMMISSION (1948-49). The Report (Chairman : Dr. Sarvapalli Radhakrishnan). P 152.
3. INDIA. UNIVERSITY GRANTS COMMISSION. Major Research Projects in Humanities and Social Sciences : A Review. *Bulletin of Higher Education*. 9; 1; April 1984 ; 1-2.
4. RAMAIAH (L.S.) and KANAKACHARY (M), *Ed*. Documentation and bibliographic control of the Humanities in India. 1992. Aditya Prakashan, Delhi.

5. STONE (Sue). Humanities scholars : information needs uses. *Journal of Documentation.* 38, 4; Dec. 1982; 293.

6. WEINTRAUB (Karl J). The Humanistic scholar and the Library. *In* Don R. Swanson (Ed). The role of libraries in the growth of knowledge : Proceedings of the 40th Conference of the Graduate Library School, May 18-19, 1979. 1980. The University of Chicago Press. Chicago- P 27.

# 17

# Collection of Cess Under the Public Libraries Act (1960) of A.P.

S.R. Ranganathan had originally suggested the Library cess in his Model Bills and Acts for library legislation on the basis of penny tax in the British Library Acts. The Library cess is a major source of income to the public libraries. Levying of cess is a common feature in most of the Library Acts passed by the Indian States except the West Bengal, Maharashtra and Mizoram Acts. The recent acts began to think about alternative sources of income to the Public Libraries.

Under Section 20 (1) of the Anclhra Pradesh Public Libraries Act of 1960, Library Cess was levied in the form of a surcharge on the property tax or house tax. In the beginning, the library cess was levied at 4 naya paise for every rupee in the property or house tax. It was enhanced to 6 paise in the Government Memorandum No.1107/Pts.lll/79.4 dated 24-9-1979. Again the cess was increased to the present rate of 8 paise.

## COLLECTION AND REMITTANCE PROCEDURE

Under Section 18(2) of the Act the cess levied shall be collected by the Municipal Corporation of Hyderabad in the twin cities, by the Municipal Council within the area of its jurisdiction, by the Gram Panchayat within its jurisdiction and by the Local Body in an area in a district not included within the jurisdiction of a Municipal Council or a Gram Panchayat.

The cess collected shall be paid in such a manner as may be prescribed to the Zilla Grandhalaya Samstha concerned.

As per Rule 18 of the Andhra Pradesh Public Libraries Rules (1961) issued in G.O.Ps.No.84 Education dated 27th March 1961, it was prescribed that the cess should be collected promptly under section 20(2) of the Act and 75% of the cess collected in a particular year be remitted to the Treasury Account of the Zilla Grandhalaya Samstha immediately after the close of the financial year and the balance of 25% be remitted after the audited figures become available.

Under Rule 18(3) of the A.P. Public Libraries Rules (1961), the Director of Municipal Administration and the Collector shall take disciplinary action against the person or persons responsible for the delay in the remittance of the cess to the Zilla Grandhalaya Samstha. The Secretary of a Zilla Grandhalaya Samstha has to report the matter to the Director of Public Libraries who shall bring it to the notice of the Director of Municipal Administration in the case of a Municipality or Municipal Corporation and the Collector in the case of any other Local Authority.

It has been stipulated in G.O.Ms. No. 391 Education (A & L) Department dated 28th October 1994 communicated to the Secretaries of all Zilla Grandhalaya Sarnsthas in the procedings No. 81-C4/92 Dated 08-11-1994 of the Director of Public Libraries that the cess collected shall be remitted in full by the Local Authorities to the Treasury Accounts of the respective Zilla Grandhalaya Samsthas within a month time from the date of collection of property tax. Afterwards the procedure to make daily remittance of library cess was brought into implementation.

## DISTRICT LEVEL REVIEW COMMITTEE

In G. O. Ms. No. 409 Education (A & L) Department dated 8th November 1994, the Government constituted the District Level Official Committee in each District to review the library cess collections with the following officers.

1. Joint Collector of the District - Chairman
2. District Panchayat Officer - Member
3. All Commissioners of the Municipalities in the District - Members
4. District Audit Officer of Local Fund Audit (Present designation: District Audit Officer, State Audit) - Member
5. Secretary, Zilla Grandhalaya Sarnstha- Member Convener

The G.O. contains mandatory direction that the Committee shall meet once in every month at district level in order to review library cess collection and to take effective steps for its payment to the Zilla Grandhalaya Samstha

## DEFAULTERS IN GUNTUR DISTRICT

In spite of all this, the Commissioners of Municipalities and Executive Officers of Panchayats are not remitting the library cess legitimately due to the Zilla Grandhalaya Samstha in the district to its Treasury Account. They are violating and flouting the statutory provision of the Public Libraries Act and Rules made thereunder. Most of the defaulters are playing dilly-dallying tactics.

It may be said that this is a fraud on the democracy. With the mounting fiscal deficit, the Zilla Grandhalaya Samsthas are finding the going difficult. It is essential to ensure prompt remittance of library cess to garner strength to the Grandhalaya

Samsthas. Then only they will be in a position to render effective modernised library service to the reading public. It is a fact that the non-remitance of library cess is a state wide problem. It is; deplorable that the Government is watching the situation as a silent spectator. Unfortunately, the officers concerned at State and District level who hasten to take disciplinary action against their subordinates for irregularities that are not so serious and are oblivious of their responsibility to prevail upon the Commissioners of Municipalities and Executive Officers and Sarpanchas of Panchayats to remit the library cess promptly and avoid default in its remittance.

In Guntur district a whopping sum of library cess arrears is due to the Zilla Grandhalaya Samstha from the Municipalities. As seen from the *praja sakthi* daily dated 15th December 2004 the Secretary of Guntur Zilla Grandhalaya Samstha gave the following information in respect of library cess due from the local bodies.

| *S.No.* | *Name of the Municipality* | *Arrears of library Cess to be remitted* |
|---|---|---|
| 1. | Tenali Municipality | Rs 45 Lakhs |
| 2. | Narasaraopet Muncipality | Rs 25 Lakhs |
| 3. | Bapatla Muncipality | Rs 8.5 Lakhs |
| 4. | Mangailagiri Municipality | Rs 11 Lakhs |
| 5. | Sathenapalli Municipality | Rs 4 Lakhs |
| 6. | Repalle Municipality | Rs 15 Lakhs |
| 7. | Macherla Municipality | Rs 62 Thousand |
| 8. | Chilakaluripet Municipality | Rs 50 Thousand |

It is learnt that in addition to the cess arrears particularised above, an amount of Rs 1,52,51,807/- (Rupees One crore Fifty Two lakhs Fifty one Thousand Eight Hundred and Seven) is due from the Municipal Corporation of Guntur to the Zilla Grandhalaya Samstha.

It cannot be said that the role of Panchayats in remitting library cess to the Zilla Grandhalaya Samstha is better. The style of functioning of some of the Panchayats is causing disappointment and despondency, lock stock and barrel. For instance the Panchayat Secretary, Village Secretariat, Duggirala of Guntur district gave information on 21-1-2003 that an amount of Rs 1,45,805 has to be paid by the Duggirala Panchayat for the years 1997-98, 1998-99, 1999-2000, 2000-01 and 2001-02, towards library cess. If the cess collections in respect of 2002-03, 2003-04 and the 9 months from April to the December ending 2004 are added to the above figure it may be said that more than Rs 2 lakhs have to be paid to the Zilla Grandhalaya Samstha, Guntur by the same Panchayat towards library cess. There is need to arrive at correct figures by adding the cess collections out of the taxes paid in E-Seva Kendras. Considerable amounts of cess are said to be due to the Zilla Grandhalaya Samstha from the Panchayats of Piduguralla and a number of other major Panchayats. It is essential that the Regional Director of Municipal Administration, the Collectorate, District Panchayat Officer and Divisional Panchayat Officers have to monitor the collections of library cess made by the Municipal Commissioners and Panchayat Secretaries and ensure prompt remittance to the Treasury Account of Zilla Grandhalaya Samstha, Guntur, as stipulated in the Public Libraries Act and Rules. Default in remittance of library cess should be a thing of the past. Delay in remitting the library cess should not be tolerated by Government. Deterrent disciplinary action should be taken against the defaulters without hesitation.

It is pertinent to state here that an amount of Rs 35.02 crores is due from the local bodies towards the arrears of library cess as on 31-03-2004. This sum has accumulated from the year 1986.

The Zilla Grandhalaya Samsthas are not able to tone up the efficiency of library service and maintain their libraries effectively for want of adequate finances. It is due to non-remittance of library cess promptly by the local bodies.

Moreover, the Government has introduced an unceremonious procedure for payment of pensionary benefits of all retired employees from the funds of the Zilla Grandhalaya Samsthas. Thus the Zilla Grandhalaya Samsthas are according to G.O. No. 915 Education dated 29th July 1975 liable for payment of pension including family pension to the retired employees of Zilla Grandhalaya Samsthas. The Government committed to pay all retirement benefits to the retired employees in the jurisdiction of the Grandhalaya Samsthas by issuing the Andhra Pradesh Zilla Grandhalaya Samsthas Employees. Pension-cum-Gratuity Fund Rules (1978) in G.O.Ms.No. 1151 Education Department dated 6th December 1978. These rules are not yet implemented though more than a quarter century passed after they were issued. The Zilla Grandhalaya Samsthas are paying the pensionary benefits, being in a state of bankruptcy subject to reimbursement by Government in the form of arrear pension grants. The Government is not reimbursing the expenditure incurred by the Zilla Grandhalaya Samsthas in time. Owing to lack of funds, the retired employees are not able to receive their benefits in time.

It is a pity rather a tragedy that in Cuddapah Zilla Grandhalaya Samstha, the employees who retired from service from June 2000 could not receive their benefits like D.C.R. Gratuity, commutation value of pension etc. till date. They are in distress. Similar situation is prevailing with slight difference in the Zilla Grardhalaya Samsthas of Nellore, Srikakulam and some other districts. The pensionary benefits of some retired employees in the Zilla Grandhalaya Sarnstha, Guntur were sanctioned. Ekit the benefits have not been paid to them for want of funds. Nearly an amount of Rs 30/- lakhs are needed to clear off the arrears of pensionary benefits in the Zilla Grandhalaya Samstha, Guntur. Though nearly an amount of Rupees one Crore and nineteen lakhs of Library Cess was received from the local bodies in 2003-04, the Zilla Grandhalaya Sarnstha, Guntur could not buy new books as the whole income was spent for payment of salaries and pensionary benefits etc. As a rule, the library cess should be utilised for development of library service only. During the present financial year (2003-2004) Rs 80 lakhs and 80 thousand of cess was received by the Zilla Grandhalaya Samstha, Guntur upto November 2004. In the present year also no new books have been purchased so far.

## PAYMENT OF INTEREST AND WASTE OF PUBLIC FUNDS

Owing to paucity of funds, the Zilla Grandhalaya Samsthas are not able to pay the pensionary benefits fully to the retired employees in time.

As per G.O. Ms. No. 268 Finance & Planning dated 7-10-1986 and G.O.Ms.No. 185 Finance & Planning dated 9-11 -1992, the reitrecl employees are entitled for interest on belated payment of D.C.R. Gratuity. In several cases interest has been paid after the beneficiaries knocked the door of the Honble Institution of Lokayukta and Upa-Lokayukta. Thus public funds are being wasted to pay interest. Recovery of the interest amount has to be made from the person or persons responsible for the late payment of D.C.R. Gratuity. But so far no such recovery has been made.

## DOUBLE STANDARDS

The Government releasing advance salary grants to the Zilla Grandhalayagram being released also is quite inadequate to pay the salaries of the staff every month. For instance an amount of Rs 7 lakhs or a few thousands more than that is given to the Zilla Grandhalaya Guntur. Samstha, Guntur as advance salary grant. But nearly Rs 14 lakhs are necessary for paying salaries every month. So, the deficit amount has to be paid by the Zilla Grandhalaya Samstha from its income received solely by way of library cess from the local bodies. It is relevant to state in this context that the Government has already committed to bear the full expenditure on salaries and pensions to the inservice and retired employees, respectively. A sum of Rs 17.95 crores has to be released to the Zilla Grandhalaya Samsthas upto to the year 2002-03 towards arrear pension grants. The Honble Chief Minister in the review meeting of the Education Department held on 8th October 2004 gave green signal for release of Rs 30 crores to meet the expenditure on payment of benefits due to the pensioners in Zilla Grandhalaya Samsthas. It is deplorable that so far the amount has not been released.

## HON'BLE LOKAYUKTA'S DIRECTIONS

In complaint No. 1098/93/B1, in the order dated 23rd March 2000 of the Honble Lokayukta, it has been stated as follows:

"It is fondly hoped by this Institution that in future the pension and salary grant would be sanctioned in advance and that in every budget proper allocations would be made and the library cess would continue to be remitted by the Local Bodies to the concerned Zilla Grandhalaya Samsthas promptly take prompt action to see that the Municipalities, Nagara Palikas and Gram Panchayats remit all the cess still due. They should try to pay this amount atleast by 30th of June, 2000." The Honble Lokayukta also gave a direction for constitution of Pension-cum-Gratuity Fund as envisaged in the A.P. Zilla Grandhalaya Samsthas Employees Pension-cum-Gratuity Fund Rules, 1978.

The Director of Public Libraries also submitted proposals to Government to sanction advance pension grant to the retired employees of Zilla Grandhalaya Samsthas. But this has not materialised.

## DIRECTOR'S LETTER TO CHIEF MINISTER'S OFFICE

An amount of Rs 12.36 crores is due from Government to Zilla Grandhalaya Samsthas in the State towards arrear pension grants as on 05-05-2003. In fact this amount was advanced by the Zilla Grandhalaya Samsthas for payment of pensionary benefits. The Director also wrote a letter No. 123-A4/2003 Dated 05-03-2003 to the Chief Minister's Office that "because of non-release of arrear pension grants and no provision for releasing advance pension grants, this problem of non-payment of pension has been perpetuating since several yeas. The only solution to this problem is to make a budget provision for payment of advance pension grant and to release pension grant," If this procedure is followed, it will ease the burden to Zilla Grandhalaya Samsthas as they need not spend any sum from their funds solely received by way of Library Cess for paying pensionary benefits.

For all this, it is essential to revamp the administration of Public Library system.

The Government should take steps to pay all the pensionary benefits to the retired employees of Zilla Grandhalaya Samsthas through Treasuries/ Banks as in the case of retired teaching and non-teaching staff of Aided Educational Institutions. It involves no additional expenditure. The Government have already committed to bear the expenditure in respect of payment of pensionary benefits.

## CONCLUSION

In a meeting held in January 1986 in the Chamber of the then Education Secretary (Sri Parthasaradhi, IAS) with Shri Kolluru Koteswara Rao Ex-M.L.C. and Editor of the *Telugu Vidyarthi* and employees representatives, Sri A. Raghavaiah offered a suggestion for prompt and full realisation of Library Cess.

The Municipalities receive entertainment tax collected by the Commercial Tax Authorities in their jurisdiction with promptitude. The Commercial Tax Officers are paying the entertainment tax collections with alacrity and without default to the Municipalities. A condition should be imposed that a Municipality or Panchayat should produce a No Due

Certificate' obtained from the Zilla Grandhalaya Samstha concerned that no Library Cess is due from the Municipality or Panchayat. Then only the entertainment tax has to oe released by Commercial Tax Authorities to the Municipality or Panchayat. This will ensure rapid remittance of Library Cess to the Zilla Grandhalaya Samsthss. This suggestion is to be examined and implemented.

It is being advocated by Library Associations and library professionals that a penal clause should be incorporated in the A.P. Public Libraries Act (1960) to take disciplinary action against the defaulters who fail to remit the cess promptly to the Zilla Grandhalaya Samsthas. In the Model Act of the Indian Library Association there is a penal clause to take action against the persons responsible for non-remittance of library cess; to the Zills. Grandhalaya Samsthas in time.

# 18

# Eleven Reasons for Reading Good Books

Reading is a private activity. It is the gateway to knowledge and wisdom. It is one of the most effective means of systematic development of the personality and language of a person. It provides access to the ideas of others cutting across the barriers of time, space and language. Reading has the unique power of transforming the readers. It is sometimes said 'that we are what we read' :

Lord Thomas B. Macaulay said : " I would rather be a poor man in a garret with planty books than a king who did not love reading." Abraham Lincoln said that "The Things I want to know are in books. My friend is the man who'll get a book I ain't read. Francies Bacon, therefore, rightly stated that "reading maketh a full man." There are as many reasons to read as there are readers. The eleven reasons identified are :

1. Reading for information
2. Reading to understand others
3. Reading to know oneself
4. Reading for fun
5. Reading for ideas
6. Reading as virtual travel

7. Reading to become a part of culture
8. Reading for suspence
9. Reading for the love of beauty
10. Reading for glimpses of perfection
11. Reading to develop thinking, writing and conversational skills.

Each of the eleven concepts are studied below in detail.

## READING FOR INFORMATION

One thinking that the modern world is full of information. A quick surf of the channels on TV or the Internet provides information on multiple subjects like laser surgery, bird behaviour, egyptology, bank rates, share markets etc. Knowledge or information that has meaning can be found in a number of places but especially in books of fiction. We find plenky of information in the novels of Charles Dickens, Tolstoy, Bernard Shaw, H.G. Wells, Mulkraj Anand, R.K. Narayan, Raja Rao etc. Similarly even in Shakespeare one can acquire practical knowledge about politics, military strategy, coinege, fabric industry, to name just a few of the subjects about which Shakespeare was particularly knowledgeble.

As Thomas Carlyle said over 150 years ago, that "The true university of these days is a collection of books." It is even more true today that almost anything a reader wants to learn about can be understood deeply and thoroughly through good books.

## READING TO UNDERSTAND OTHERS

Reading books provide ample opportunity to understand various races, countries, environments, people, their habits, cultures, festivals, dresses etc. Particularly literature books are enjoyable because they are about human beings. Literature presents many typical human situations and a wide sampling of the ways different people have tried to deal with them. The more we have read, the more likely that we will be prepared to deal with new and unusual situations in our own lives. The more options that we are aware of, the more people we have read about and know intimately. The more likely that we will be capable of dealing with others.

Through reading we can explore the psychologies of others. Reading Somerset Maugham's *Of Human Bondage* enables us to understand human psychology. Characters in various novels reveal to readers different paths of life and act like guides to understand others.

## READING TO KNOW ONESELF

Socraes and even *Bhagavad Gita* said, 'Knowledge', it is a simple formulation, difficult of execution. People scramble from crisis to crisis, without any self-awareness or principles to guide them on the religious side, There are many *Ashramas*, Churches and Mosques waiting to guide people. On the secular side, literature can be a huge help. In the words of Clifton Fadiman, "When you re-read a classic you do not see more in the books than you did before; you see more in you than there was before."

Reading good books encourages the readers to identify and enrich their authentic interests. Books give readers a chance to ask, over and over again, in hypothetical situations what would they do, Reading is also a way of putting peoples lives and selves in proper perspective. Reading about people whose lives are more deprived, more damaged than ours can make us appreciate the things that we can be thankful for. Reading is a sure way of fitting ourselves into the hierarchy of things and seeing where we stand, and if that is where we want to stand.

## READING FOR FUN

Ironically, many students learn to dislike reading right in school because of out dated courses mandated by the educational authorities. Students bogged down with continued assignments, hardly get a chance to read books that appeal to their adolescent sensibilities or to explore their own particular youthful interest. No wonder nobody because of the tight schedule of curriculum and competition is having any fun. There are plenty of wonderful authors who tackle serious questions in amusing ways.

Humour itself is a topic of incredible interest, as it is well known that one person's hysterical joke is another person's burning nighmare. Finding the relevant authors is part of the enjoyment of reading. Holbook Jackson in his book. *The Anatomy of Bibliomania* said, "Books are never out of humour, never envious or Jealous, they answer all questions with readiness ... They dispel melancholy by their mirth, and amuse by their wit."

## READING FOR IDEAS

Some people are genuinely interested in big ideas. They have a theoretical bent that might be satisfied by reading the great philosphers, the important social thinkers or the important works of world religions. Other people like to explore the big ideas through the microcosm of individual lives. Book reading is the natural path to metaphysics to them.

Every person has his own personal philosophy, inspite of it one can always explore the ideas of others as expressed in their works. The works of Thomas Hardy, Camus and Jean Paul Sartre contain ideas on philosophy of predestination and existentalism respectively. Most philosophers have turned, at one time or another, to story telling to make their ideas accessible to more people. Jesus, Buddha and Mohammed all told stories to their disciples to help, clarify and spread their ideas.

Old books and new books are all full of so many remarkable ideas. Books are written and published only to spread ideas universally.

## READING AS VIRTUAL TRAVEL

Through reading books dealing with travel, it is possible to escape the boundaries of geography and travel virtually anywhere, anytime. The books of Ernest Hemingway, and Henry James show us Spain and England respectively. Their description of full lights and drawing rooms are vivid. Victor Hugo's book, *The Hunchback of Notre Dame* displays to the readers the ninteenth century Paris. It is in this context only, Thomas Carlyle said that "In books lies the soul of the whole past time." People by reading books can know ahead about the places actually they are travelling to. The use of travel literature shall enhance one's travel experience and open a window onto the entire world.

## READING TO BECOME A PART OF CULTURE

More the people read, the more they become part of their culture and also form an important of the process of transmitting that culture to the next generation. Books are the carriers of civilization. Without books history is silent, literature dumb and thought and speculation at a standstill.

Full cultural participation requires some familiarity with the classic such as the *Ramayana*, the *Mahabharata*, the *Gita Govindam*, and Kalidas's *Shakuntalam* etc. There are basic texts of western literature that every reader would do well to know. To give only few examples : Shakespear's *Hamlet*, Sophocle's *Antigone*, Dante's *Divine Comedy*, Chaucer's *Canterbery Tales* Gibbon's *Decline and Fall of the Roman Empire*, Heny Jame's *Portrait of a Lady*, Milton's *paradise lost*, Tolstoy's *war and peace* Dostoyesky's *Crime and Punishment*, Thoreau's *walden* etc. Every language and country have their own classics which should be read, chewed and digested.

Finally, there is an interplay between literature and other arts. Literature makes music, theatre, painting, sculpture, architecture and media more enjoyable and meaningful.

Reading such literature bring us into the cultural mix and keep the identity of the readers.

## READING FOR SUSPENSE

Detective or mystery novels provide a rich share of literature. Suspense is their quality that makes it difficult to put a book down. Curiosity leads readers from page to page with anxiety and excitement. Agatha Christie, *The Murder of Rogu Ackroyal* is one such novel. *Vikram and the Vempire* keeps. The suspense of the readers with an axiety to know what happens next. A good example of the suspense literature is the classic and the *Thousand* and *one Nights*. In this the king shahryar is kept in suspense by Sharazad telling a stroy every night and stop her tale at the most suspenseful moment and keeps the king to know that he/be told the ending of the story the following night. The story goes on like that. There are readers who anxiously await for the publication of such literature.

## READING FOR THE LOVE OF BEAUTY

Keats said that "a thing of beauty is Joy forever." Words, ofcourse, are everyone's common property but the order of words often has magic in them. There is aesthetic beauty of a well turned phrase and the arabesque intricacies of a plot in a novel. There are masters of style. The pure beauty of the book's language or form makes readers to read and re-read them many times from young age to old age.

The Peotry of Ghalib, Keats, Shelly etc. take people into mental esctasy. The works of Premchand, Bankim, Cervantes, Virginia Woolf, and many more English novelists and dramtists have beauty in language, plot, form and style which keep readers awstruck and spellbound. The beauty of certain books fill the hearts of readers with joy. It is with the reading of books the same as with looking at pictures, one must, without a doubt, without hesitations, with assurance, and admire what is beautiful.

## READING FOR GLIMPSES OF PERFECTION

Most religions caution people that perfection does not exist on earth but they also hold out perfection as a worthy goal to strive toward. They frequently describe an other worldly after life where perfection will finally be realised by various followers. There is certainly a yearning in the human heart for glimpses of a perfect world and universe.

A large body of works in literature is a product of this impulse to glimpse the flawless. Plato tried to imagine a perfect state in his book, *The Republic*. Different people have different ideas about what a perfect society or life, might look like. Thoreau in his book *Walden Pond*, B.F. Skinner in his book *Walden Two* had tried to create a society in which many people can live in harmony. Karl Marx and Huxley approached the problem of perfect society in a different way. Many writers have tried to point the direction to perfection by exploring inperfection. Orwell's 1984 is an another work which tried to describe another model of society. It is difficult to visualise glimpses of perfect society. Only in books mankind has known perfect truth, love and beauty. Reading vast uptopian literature, people aspire to find glimpses of perfection which is like will-o-the whisp.

## READING TO DEVELOP THINKING, WRITING AND CONVERSATIONAL SKILLS

**1. Thinking :** Reading literature cultivates the vanishing ability to pay attention, and think choerently. There are many enemies of attention in the modern world such as cricket, game shows, commercials, stock market etc. These are all hinderences to thinking in this age of inattention. Reading forces the readers to use their faculties of imagination. Like all other faculties, imagination is enhanced, through constant use, and a well exercised imagination can be an asset in almost any setting. Reading different types of books provide the readers with basic raw materials for imagination and thinking. Basically the human being is a thinking animal and the reading specially a good schedule enhances the thinking power.

**2. Writing :** Generally people read because they want to write. A great many readers eventually try their hand at writing or are inspired to write by something they have read. Reading is a great generator of ideas, a tremendous motivation to express their ideas. Reading enhances the reader's vocubalaries, sharpens their minds and activates their imagination and creative abilities. Reading helps people in selecting the right word and right argument to putting their ideas and feelings correctly across to others. Reading helps the fluency of speaking of the readers.

**3. Conversation :** There is inseperable relationship between reading, writing and conversation. Kosta Bagakis a Czech Writer in his book, *Speaking of Reading* says: "I maintain that reading is a social act. A book won't stay in my head unless I tell a friend about it, so I like to find other people to read the books I'm reading so we can talk about the ideas together. Sometimes it's if we've read different books, our ideas are so different. I have never read a book without sharing it with others – never." Conversationists are appreaciated for their ability in keeping the people awe struck with their sweet tongue. Reading aids the ability of conversation with fun and fluency. It is always joy to sit with people who had wide reading and discuss with them about writers and their works.

## CONCLUSION

Reading makes a person liberal and democrat. People who don't read are like dumb animals. Bacon is absolutely correct when he says that "Reading maketh a full man." People read poetry and fiction for all kinds of reasons – all of them good. Here are a number of valid reasons to pursue a reading life, from same noteworthy authors.

**Isabel Allende :** "For me life without reading would be like being in prison, it would be as it my spirit were in a strait Jacket life would be a very dark and narrow place."

**Alan Bloom** : "The failure to read good books both enbables the vision and strengthens our most fatal tendency – the belicf that the here and now is there is."

**Charles de Secondar** : "I've never known any trouble that an hours reading didn't assuage."

**Sir Richard Steele** : "Reading is to the mind what exercise is to the body."

**Michel de Montaigne** : "When I am attacked by gloomy thoughts, nothing helps me so much as running to my books. They quickly absorb me and banish the clouds from my mind."

**Franz Kafka** : "A book must be the axe for the frozen sea within us."

**Jean Paul Sartre** : "All that I know about my life, it seems I have learned from books."

**Ezra Pound** : "If a nation's literature declines, the nation atrophies and decays."

**Edmund Burke** : "To read without reflecting is like eating without digesting."

**Joseph Brodsky** : "There are worse erimes than burning books : one of them is not reading them."

**Cicero** : "To add a library to a house is to give that house a soul."

## BIBLIOGRAPHY

1. BAMBERGER, Richard (1975) Promoting the reading habit. Paris, Unesco.
2. HASAN, Abur (1973) Promoting the reading habit IN Priorities and planning for the provision of books. London, Commonwealth Secretariat. P. 75–79.
3. MANN, Peter (1982) From author to reader : A social study of books. London : Routledge and Kegan paul.

4. MANN, Peter and BURGOYNE, Jacquiline (1969) Books and reading. London : Andre Deutsch.

5. McLELLEN, A.W. (1973) The reader, the library and the book London, Clive Bingley.

6. RAMAIAH, L.S., (1990) "To make reading a habit, way of life. "*The Hindu*, 16th October.p.19.

7. SWINGEWOOD, Alan (1977) The myth of mass cultures. London, Macmillian.

8. WILSON, Douglas L (1994), "What Jefferson and Lincoln read." *Span* 35 : 2. pp 2–9.

# 19

# Trends in Information Technology : An Overview

## INTRODUCTION

Information Technology(IT) is a generic term that covers the acquisition, processing, storage and dissemination of information. It covers the application of computers, communication technology, telecommunications in the tasks of information handling and information flow from the generation to the utilization levels. It is restricted to systems dependent on micro-electronics based combination of computers and telecommunication.

The UNESCO defines IT as Scientific, Technological and Engineering disciplines and the management techniques used in information handling and processing, their applications, computers and their interaction with men and machines, and associated social, economic and cultural matters.

Information Technology is having a more profound effect because, in principle, it overcomes the space barrier for a much larger range of informative messages and greatly reduces the need for local information stores. There is now a possibility of immediate access by each individual to all intermediate sources and even to original sources of information.

IT increases capacity for knowledge gathering. Knowledge is like light, weightless and intangible. It can easily travel across the world enlightening the lives of the people everywhere. It begins with the realization that economies are built not merely through accumulation of physical capital and human skills, but on a foundation of information, learning and adaptation. It revolutionized human life across globe. Now, people even from remote villages do have fast access to knowledge available in any corner of the world at a nominal cost. Still millions of people are living in darkness and poverty. Now the difference between the rich and poor is not only of the amount of wealth and capital, but also of information and knowledge. Creation of knowledge is still expensive but IT has made its availability cheaper. It helps not only in the spread of knowledge but also in its creaton.

The facilities required to capture, store, manipulate and distribute data and information, could broadly be called as Information Technology. Contrary to popular misconception, IT is not just computers, although they form a major part of it. IT consists of the following :

**(a) Computers :** This is a central component of IT and ranges from microchip based personal computers to supercomputers. It also includes minicomputers, mainframes and workstations. Revolutionary technologies like RISC are making computers more compact and power packed.

**(b) Telecommunications :** With recent advancements in the digital telecommunications field, this has become a critical partner in the IT area. By networking computers across geographical and organizational boundaries and linking customers/suppliers with the organization, the power of the computers is multiplied manifold. State of the technology includes digital switching and equipment which rely on fiber optics and satellites for actual transmission, Electronic Data

Interchange, Integrated digital services Networking and Video-conferencing.

Industrial Revolution has given us production technologies which have revolutionized methods of production. It has given us better quality products at more competitive prices. In some cases, it has given products which did not exist earlier. Today, IT is bringing about a similar revolution in the methods of business and management, which the industrial technology brought in the methods of production. That is why it has been called as the Second Industrial Revolution.

The term IT has come into common use since the mid-80s with the integration of the computer technology, and the communication technology. Today IT provides integrated solutions for development of information systems in organizations and society. Information system is the nervous system of any organization and *sine quanon* for its survival.

It is an integrated technology, which includes within its sphere computer, telecommunication and broadcasting products by recognizing the technological convergence of these three fields. Computer is the core of IT world, which has indeed gained much popularity in almost every span of life. Everywhere we witness the elegance, sophistication and efficiency possible only with the help of computers. Advantages flowing from IT are as follows:

1. Provides different services at one window often called single window clearance.
2. Flattens organizational structure
3. Speeds up operations and saves time
4. Reduces paper work, and
5. Improves team performance

## TYPES OF MANAGEMENT INFORMATION SYSTEMS

Information systems that support managerial functions in the organization are Management Information Systems.

(MIS). These are designed to generate information that helps management decision-making. The information generated may be suggestive, predictive, decisive or systematic. The information systems are classified into Databank Information System, Predictive Information System, Decision-making Information System and Decision Taking Information system.

**Trends in applications of IT** : The application of IT in India was characterized by the population census compilation in the 60s, airlines reservation in the 70s, railway reservation in the 80s and Stock exchange trading in the 90s. Electronic Commerce, Electronic Banking and Electronic Data Interchange are already widespread In developed countries. For example, if you open an account in a British Bank, you are not merely the customer of the bank branch where you open the account, but a customer of the bank as a whole. You can see your balance or withdraw money from your account from any ATM of the bank anywhere in the country.

Internet and intranets have opened new frontiers of IT application. Flow of information within the organization and also from various external sources has become very smooth and instantaneous. Managers in the organization can retrieve data from internal external databases and process it for decision-making according to their requirements without delay. Even the physical movement of managers does not effect the information flow. Successful IT application is always a result of joint co-operative effort of IT system designers and user managers. The analyst designer and the user have to work together for successful implementation of IT based system. We need to have managers with good understanding of IT and IT professionals with good understanding of business and management.

## AREAS OF IT APPLICATIONS

Urban Services Development of an on-line integrated information and monitoring system for delivery, accounting, compliance, and payment for services like water supply, electricity, telephones, etc. The following are the areas where IT applications can be applied successfully

1. Compliance and payment of taxes
2. Filing of complaints
3. Managing Traffic on the roads
4. Development projects
5. Social security of employees
6. Managing imports and exports cargo
7. Payment of bills and booking passage
8. Appointment and transfer of personnel
9. Checking unauthorized construction

**Some Success Stories**

Some examples of computerization that have tremendously improved the efficiency of the economy are cited below.

1. The Indian railways have introduced an online passenger reservation system where tickets can be issued for any train, class, and destination on any day based on any criteria. The online-booking system has the greatest advantage in terms of getting return journey reservation as well. Reaching his destination, a passenger is no longer pre-occupied with the tension of arranging his return journey. Now, he can concentrate more on the job in hand. A cost-benefit study under the aegis of Ministry of Information Technology, revealed that there is a large saving in the daily queuing hours for passengers. At the same time, the booking clerks have savings in routine chores, such as elaborate tallying of cash. Also, Indian railways have set up information kiosks in Mumbai, New Delhi, Bangalore and other cities. These kiosks will initially provide reservation status and train schedules. Indian railways has a vast cable network that may be

utilized by way of offering it on lease to Internet service Providers.

2. The Uttar Pradesh State electricity Board and many other state electricity authorities run computer base billing systems. This conversion from the earlier manual system, an internal study of the UPSEB showed, brought a gain in revenue which is running into several crores in the initial efforts for the western UP districts computerization alone.

3. The Indian police in around 16 states have introduced computerization in the crime-criminal information system considering that about 20 per cent of the crimes are of inter-district and other 20 per cent are of inter-state kind. A quick linkage and matching of the suspects with the extent records maintained by the human "Collators" at each remote police station and centralized at the district headquarters has helped to bring the guilty to book speedily.

4. In recent past, a task force on IT was constituted and its recommendations reached the people in no time. IT enable people to enrich this important document by online adding of their personal opinions, observations, comments and suggestions.

5. The vigilance commission has also used the WWW technology, making people more conscious of their rights and duties in fighting corruption. The commission has displayed the names of corrupt government officers and public servants on its website disgracing them openly in the public. It's a highly appreciated and recommendable step at a point of time when the nation is passing through a rough weather in combating poverty, unemployment, corruption, terrorism, and social insecurity.

## Recent Trends

The personal computer revolution happened and it has

affected millions of lives. It has led us to places we had barely imagined through web-sites and Internet connections. There have been several major shifts in the last five years that are bound to influence the way we live and conduct business. Though, in recent past, computers have been used largely for data processing, their role in the years to come will be In exciting areas like telecommunications, e-mail, and image processing. This new area, called Integrated Services Digital Network (ISDN) promises to be the most revolutionary development, since the development of computers. Further, these developments herald the arrival of a true information society as follows.

1. The Internet and the WWW have brought the any time any where paradigm to consumers allowing them to conduct their transactions at their convenience . These technologies have also enabled round the clock access to distant expertise and knowledge.
2. The distributed-processing model, based on inexpensive but powerful networked computers, has the potential to bring the power of computing to large resource-scarce countries. Thus, every village, school, small business, public service organizations—like hospital and public offices—could access information and knowledge available anywhere in the country.
3. The ministers may open their web-sites that will help citizens to put forth their views. Ministers can display the steps taken for the benefits of various sections of society on these sites. The performance indicators of the economy policy statements, circulars etc. can also be made known. This mode of dissemination of Information will be of great help *to* the Industry. Some such sites already exist today. But there is little—and often irrelevant -information on the websites of most ministers. The sites should be updated continuously so that no stale information is disseminated.

4. With the internet as a catalyst , way of working is likely to change more in the next 10 years than it has in the last 50 years. The Internet connects everything and every one. Beyond providing an inexpensive and standard way to link computing systems together, it also puts vast amounts of valuable information within easy reach. By allowing any one to instantly interact with the administration, the Internet can flatten an organizational structure and remove traditional hierarchical barriers.

## ACTIVE ROLE FOR THE GOVERNMENT

IT is an essential pre-requisite for providing basic infrastructure inputs to secure the desired industrial development and economic progress. Adequate dissemination of information is essential for social change. It is important to understand the role of information as a raw material for development. Government understands the enormous potential of IT not only as a tool for improving governance and creating more jobs, but more significantly as a means to greatly enhance the standard of living of the people. Use of IT in enhancing the delivery of government services leads to a very responsive and transparent administration, facilitating empowerment of people and satisfying their right of information. Computers, as a vital link in IT are essential for securing administrative reforms at all levels of management.

By developing integrated IT based frameworks, government can rapidly change its non-performing image only to become popular super performers. At state and local levels, the government is trying to use IT to be more efficient and cost-effective.

Societies today are multi-cultural and multi-racial, more conscious of age, religion and gender than ever before. Social issues are complex and citizens are demanding a greater diversity of public services. They are not interested in which public official a responsible for what public service. They will rather have every thing available from one integrated source.

## Some Suggestions to Enhance IT Applications

1. IT must play a role at all levels of management which is both pervasive and persistent. The benefits derived from IT should not be confined to a particular group or level of management. Efforts at all levels of management should be systematically synchronized and co-ordinated. Management comprises three levels: operational, tactic, and executive (in ascending order).The data requirement varies with the level of management. As one moves up the hierarchy, the data gets filtered and in the process quantification of data is reduced but its quality is enhanced. At operational level, a manager deals with voluminous data , but at the highest level, a manager is interested in reports, forms, and information and not the data.The application of IT should thus be consistent with the goals and objectives of management.
2. Emphasis should be on IT training rather than on IT education. IT education is concerned more about IT products and IT software industry, while IT training is all about the use of the IT product and IT software for application by software developers and computer users in specific fields, who can make official and business systems more efficient and cost-effective. One of the returns to an organization for its investment in training employees is in terms of winning over customers by rendering quality services to them. Quality services mean "Right Services at the Right Time at the Right Cost". The government and public works department must understand the importance of training and keep abreast its workforce with the skills of providing quality services.
3. So far , in general, policy-making in the area of spreading information and knowledge in the field of telecommunication and computers has been looked at

from technical angles only. The right type of thrust is still lacking. One has to look at specific application areas of IT that can make a real impact on the Indian scene during the next two decades.

4. Having recognized the potential areas, the contents and subject matter to be made available through these technologies must be consistent with the need of different categories of users, their information seeking behaviour, capability of assimilation of information and application to their different tasks.

5. The officers should be linked by network, and the businessmen may get a single-window clearance, if at all they are required to physically go to the office with some proposal. The object of every innovation in the technology is to provide increased productivity with ease and comfort to human beings.

6. In a world dominated by Information and Communication technology (ICTs), survival demands that one's skills are ICT friendly and the products one makes are designed or manufactured with ICT-friendly processes. This does not imply that every one should acquire the specialized competencies of a software engineer or a programmer. India's economy needs people specialized in a variety of skills and conversant with the use of modern tools in their own varied specialization, ie., in a specific domain giving a wider perspective.

7. Schools need to shift from mere teaching technology to teaching application of technology as well. As Dr S. Radhakrishnan aptly observed: "Education must make our people the masters of technology and not it's slave". Truly multi-disciplinary education is involved in preparing young people to use modern tools in their own fields of enterprise, and to compete with others In the world in a global market. For instance, proper exploitation of the WWW technology demands expertise in commerce,

design, arts, advertising and marketing.

8. It is well known that a product is the combined effort of processes and people who apply these processes. We are, therefore, required to duly emphasis the importance of people in the whole process. Small may be beautiful, but not in the IT industry. In the knowledge era and a skill-based economy, it has become imperative that human resource is one of the most essential ingredients of success. The growth of IT companies world wide depends on its people and the intellectual capital it possesses.

9. Instead of keeping pace with or getting swayed by the latest in hardware and software, the concerned authorities should rather concentrate on the optimum utilization of the given resources. New technologies always generate hype and often leave the impact on the society in more than one way. Experiment with the new may be made only when existing and available resources have been optimally utilized and fully exploited.

## WIDENING IT APPLICATIONS IN INDIA

The changes occurring in the field of computer technology and telecommunications over the last many years provided the base for big revolution in IT. There has been exponential growth in the volume of information and its processing. Collection, processing and dissemination of knowledge, data and information through the internet now are a routine business. It is difficult to imagine an economy to function without the use of internet. E-commerce and E-business and E-learning types of things have taken over the traditional economic and commercial activities. All these transactions are being carried out at a very low cost. It has revolutionized the economic world. IT has particularly revolutionized the transport, communication, trade, banking, education and medical sectors of the economy.

## IT AND GOOD GOVERNANCE

Good governance itself depends on a range of factors-including administrative capacity, the country's stage of development, the external conditions that it faces and the state of IT available to it for taking decisions. Governance is often described as good governance of society. Good governance has many dimensions, (a) the just exercise of authority, (b) the problem solving and conflict resolving capacity, and (c) the efficient performance of its functions based on involvement of a societal coalition for development. The role of IT in improving the governance is manifolds as follows.

1. It helps in improving the management of public resources
2. It supports development and maintenance of a transparent and stable economic and regulatory environment, conducive to efficient private sector activities (for example, price systems, exchange and trade regimes and banking systems and their related regulations)
3. It helps in institutional reforms of treasury, budget preparation and approval procedures, tax administration, accounting and audit mechanisms, central bank operations, and official statistical function.
4. It injects efficiency and transparency into the entire economic reform programme presently being implemented in many countries, including India.

## CONCLUSION

Now the computers are finding increasing usage in all aspects of government functioning. Management Information Systems are being developed to assist the decision making at various levels of administration. The era of Informatics in the government seems to have really begun. Taking up computerization in the areas which directly benefit the public and provides better and efficient services to them will create a general awareness in the minds of the public about the utility of computers. The live example is computerization of railway reservation and Indian airlines. Definitely, these projects have created a positive atmosphere in the minds of the public. Computerised billing of telephone, water, electricity services etc. will further create favourable response from the public and there will be a general psychological pressure on the Government for introducing computers in such areas.

Wide use of IT is likely to affect all the aspects of administration culture by making people's access to data and information . IT would be the instrument for transforming the nature and style of India's public administration into a participative culture, taking the people as partners in development administration.

# Index

## (It is Name and Subject Index)

### A



### B



### C